世界に誇れる盲偉人 杉山和一
―江戸期に視覚障害者の職業教育施設を開校

今村鎭夫／文　吉澤みか／絵

　江戸時代に入ってまもない1610年（慶長15年）、伊勢の国の安濃津（現在の三重県津市）の城主・藤堂高虎に仕える、杉山権右衛門重政というさむらいの家に、賢そうな男の子が生まれました。

　男の子は、養慶と名づけられ、武家の男子として大切に育てられました。

「養慶さまは本当に素直で元気な子だから、杉山家は幸せじゃ……」と、まわりの人たちからも言われ

ていました。

　ところが数え7歳となった年、これまで病気一つしなかった養慶が、国中で大流行していた疱瘡にかかってしまいました。当時は疱瘡が原因で死ぬ人も多かったのですが、養慶は両親の懸命な看護のおかげで命は助かりました。しかし、その高熱により目が見えなくなってしまったのです。

母親にだっこされ、うれしそうな赤ん坊の養慶。

「ああ、かわいそうなことをしてしまった。私が代われるものなら代わってあげたい……」

母親は、養慶を連れて目に良いといわれるお医者さまや、目を治すといわれているお寺や神社を訪ね歩きました。

しかし、両親の必死な願いにもかかわらず、目は見えるようにはなりません。

そんなある日、父・重政は、母親を呼んでいいました。

「養慶が助かったのは良かったが、目が見えなくては武家の後継ぎにはできないのだ。お寺に頼んで、仏門につかえさせるのも一つかもしれないが……」

「どうしたら、よろしいのでしょうか」

「我が家では身体の不自由な息子一人ぐらいは養えないことはない。ただ、何の目的もなしに生きてゆくことだけはさせたくない」

「わたくしもそのように思います」

母親が見守るなか、医者に目のようすをみてもらう養慶。

　養慶の両親は、かれの将来のことを考えて、何よりも自立心を育てようと決めました。

　目が見えないことを理由に人に甘えることのない心を育てようと、厳しくしつけることにしたのです。

　自分できちんと着物を着たり、人から笑われないような行儀を身につけたりすることを第一に教えました。

　しかし、養慶は、両親の思いを理解できず、
「見えないので、できないのです」
　と、なんでも親に助けを求めます。
「時間がかかっても自分でやりなさい。あなたに教えることはしても、手伝ってはあげません」
　母親は、手を貸すことはしません。養慶が泣いたりあばれたりしても、けっしてかれの言いなりにはなりません。どんなことでも自分の力でやりぬくことができるような人間になってほしいと願っていたからです。

　両親の厳しいしつけと優しい心配りのおかげで、養慶はしだいにたくましく成長していきました。

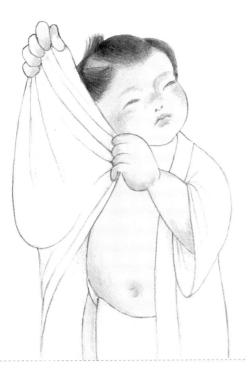

右上は、幼いころの、泣いてだだをこねている養慶。左下は、ひとりで着替えができるようになった養慶。
中央には、武士の子として立派な成長をとげた養慶がいる。

やがて、養慶が18歳になったころ、両親に言いました。

「目が不自由になったのですから、さむらいの道はあきらめます。かといって、琴、三味線で身を立てる自信はありません。そのかわり、江戸（現在の東京都）に、山瀬琢一という近頃評判の盲人の鍼医がいることを知りました。できたらその方の弟子になり、病気で苦しんでいる人たちを助けてあげたいのです」

当時は盲人の仕事といえば琵琶法師か三味線弾き、あん摩と決まっていました。鍼医などはあまりなかった時代です。しかし、昔病気をしたときに鍼を受けた経験から、養慶は、鍼治療で身を立て、刀を捨てて一人の盲人として生きる決心を告げたのです。

「二度とわが家の敷居をまたがないというぐらいの覚悟があるのなら、留めはしない」

両親の許しを得た養慶は、苦労をしながら江戸までたどり着き、芝の愛宕下（現在の東京都港区）にある山瀬琢一の治療所を訪ねて、弟子にしてくださいと頼みました。

当時、盲人の鍼医はほとんどいませんでした。琢一は師匠とはいえ、まだ30歳ぐらいの鍼医です。

鍼術で多くの病に苦しむ人を救いたいという養慶の純粋な心意気に感動した琢一は、すぐに入門を許してくれました。そして、養慶は、自分の名を、当時の盲人の琵琶法師に名づける「一」を付して「和一」と改め、決意も新たにするのでした。

（上）経絡から広がる人体の宇宙に思いをはせる養慶の横顔。
（右下）杖を頼りに、旅姿で江戸へと向かう養慶。

　そのころは、技術を習うために内弟子といって師匠の家に住み込み、弟子は師匠の身のまわりの世話から水くみや掃除もやらなければなりません。しかもこのとき、内弟子というのは和一ひとり。

　自宅とは違ったしきたりに合わせて掃除、洗濯、部屋の整理、加えて患者の受付と、多くの仕事をするのは大変なことでした。

　ある日、師匠と二人で遅い夕食をとっていたときのことです。

「和一、お前、疲れているのかい。仕事が雑でおそいぞ。床掃除に手を抜いていないかい」

「いえ、そんなつもりはありません……」

「わしは、目は見えないが、足の裏にも目があるのじゃ。嘘はつけんぞ」

　この言葉を聞いて、和一は師匠が鍼治療の技術だけがすぐれているのではないことを知りました。それからは、和一は部屋の掃除をしたあと、必ず自分の手や足の裏でゴミが残っていないかどうか確かめるようになりました。

長い廊下をひとりでぞうきん掛けする和一。廊下の端に師匠が立っている。

5

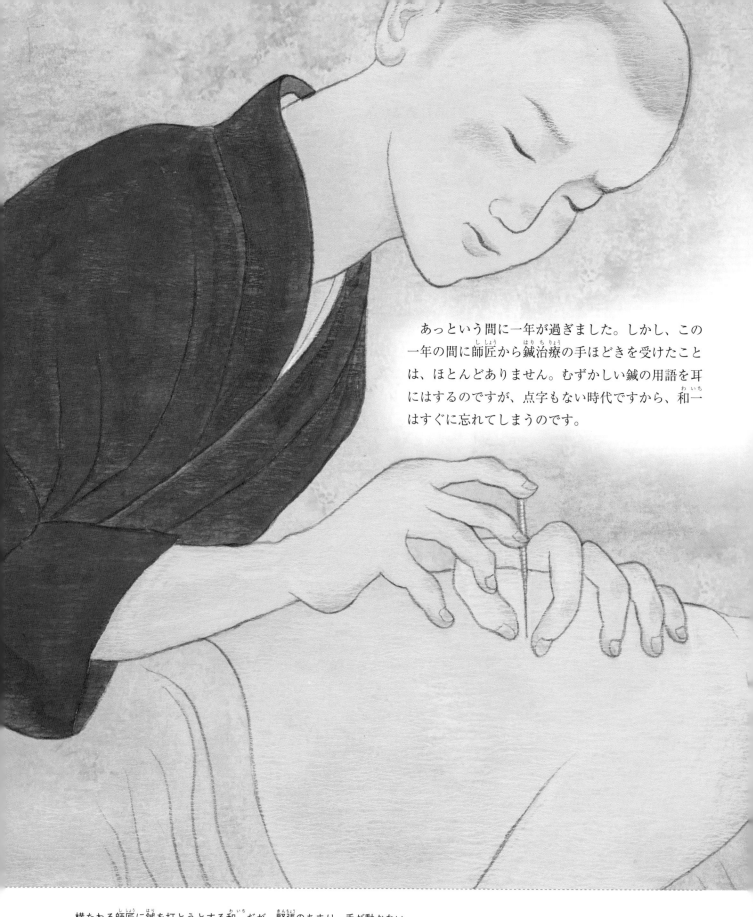

あっという間に一年が過ぎました。しかし、この一年の間に師匠から鍼治療の手ほどきを受けたことは、ほとんどありません。むずかしい鍼の用語を耳にはするのですが、点字もない時代ですから、和一はすぐに忘れてしまうのです。

横たわる師匠に鍼を打とうとする和一だが、緊張のあまり、手が動かない。

2年目を迎えたころから、和一の心のなかに不安が生まれました。

—今日も師匠は何も教えてくださらなかった。内弟子とは名ばかりで雑用係ではないだろうか—

でも、両親との固い約束があるので、弱音を吐くわけにはいきません。

3年目を過ぎた春の初めのころ、突然、和一は師匠に呼ばれました。

「今日は少し時間があるので、ひとつ、わしに鍼を打ってみなさい」

「えっ？　師匠の身体にでしょうか」

あまりにも突然のことでしたから、和一はうれしいというより、緊張のあまり頭のなかがぼうっとなってしまいました。

「師匠、何も教えていただいていないので、できません。どこに打てばよいのでしょうか」

すると、師匠は今まで聞いたことがないような大声で和一をどなりつけました。

「今なんと言った。教わっていないと申したな。お前は毎日、雑用ばかりさせられていると、不満をもって3年間を過ごしてきたのか」

「いえ……」

口ごもってうち消したものの、師匠は和一の心の中を見通していました。

「ここには、毎日、大勢の患者さんが治療を受けにやってくる。わしは患者さんとやりとりをしながら、治療している。お前は住み込んでいるのだから、朝早くから夜おそくまで、学ぶ機会は限りなくあるはずだ」

「……」

「お前に家の中の仕事をさせていたのは、雑用係として利用しているのではないのだ。仮に鍼治療の腕が良くても、人として尊敬されなければ社会では通用しないぞ」

師匠の言葉に、和一は自分が浅はかだったことを深く恥じて反省しました。

鍼治療は、人間の複雑な身体のなりたちを知ることから始まり、たくさんの医療の用語を覚えなければならないのですから、簡単ではありません。師匠もそれからは、わずかな時間をさいて教えてくれるようになったのですが、和一はなかなか覚えられません。

師匠が自らの身体に鍼を打たせるのですが、和一は緊張しすぎてうまく鍼が打てません。師匠は内心、和一の将来に不安を感じるようになりました。しかし、大きな夢を描いている和一を預かったという責任もあったので、鍼治療の実技を身に付けさせようと努力しました。でも、和一は、一向に上達しないどころか、あとから入門してきた弟子に先を越されてしまうのです。

内弟子生活も5年を過ぎたある日、和一は師匠から部屋に呼ばれました。

「和一や！　わしは、ずいぶん時間をかけてお前を指導してきたつもりだが、これ以上は無理だ。いくら教えても、痛みを感じない鍼が打てるようにならない。

わしは、自分なりの方法で技術を身につけた。お前が望むような技術をわしは持ち合わせてはいない。そこでまことに冷たいようだが、明日にでも荷物をまとめ、ここを引き上げて親元へ帰りなさい」

この突然の申し渡しに、和一は、ただ茫然としながらも、なんとか続けてくださいとお願いしました。しかし、許されることはありませんでした。

一睡もできずに朝を迎えた和一は、師匠にお別れの挨拶をしました。

「和一、わしにはできないが、工夫次第で、おまえが思うような鍼治療ができるはずだ。あとは、お前の努力と、それに『神仏のお力』も忘れてはならないぞ」

「長いことお世話になりました」

あふれ出る涙を拭い、5年間お世話になった師匠の家を出たのは、春も浅い4月の初旬でした。道案内をしてくれる人もいません。いまさらおめおめと故郷に帰ることもできません。

―さあ、どこに行こう？　どうしたら良いだろう？―

途方にくれていたときです。和一は、ふと師匠が別れる直前にいわれた「神仏のお力」という一言を思い出しました。

和一は、もはや神仏に頼るほかはないと、当時古くから盲人の守護神と崇められていた江ノ島の弁天さまにお願いに行こうと決心しました。江ノ島は相模の国（現在の神奈川県）の藤沢にある小さな島ですが、日本三大弁天として有名で、手の技の神さまとして祀られていました。

でも、江ノ島へ行く道がわかりません。木の杖を頼りに道で出会った人に聞きながら南へ歩いていくことにしました。

江戸の街は人通りも多く、行く先を尋ねると、たいていの人が親切に教えてくれました。なかには盲人とわかると、わざわざ手をひいてくれる人もいました。しかし、逆に、「おいおい、何をうろうろ歩いているんだよ」と、まるで邪魔者あつかいにして暴言を浴びせる人もいました。

お寺の住職が用意してくれた夕ごはんをいただく和一。うれしさで顔に笑みがうかぶ。

　江戸から江ノ島までの距離は十数里（約50キロメートル）ほど。しかし、東海道といっても、当時は土と石ころを踏み固めたようなデコボコ道です。おまけに道中には、追剥や盗人がいて、とても危険です。

　和一は雨さえ降らなければ、日中は杖を頼りに歩き、夜は安宿に泊まりました。

　師匠からいただいたお餞別は大切につかわなければなりません。節約をするため、だんだんとお寺や神社に泊めてもらうことが多くなりました。

　ときにはお寺の住職から夕食をふるまわれて、心温まる思いをしたり、親切なかご屋さんに出会って、ただで乗せてもらったりすることもありました。しかし、道に迷い、民家で道を尋ねて追い払われたことや、雷にあって怖い思いをしながらも歩き続け、石につまずきけがをして、朝はいた草鞋が夕方にはボロボロになっていることもありました。

　およそ5、6日間をかけ、和一は江ノ島にたどり着きました。

　風呂にも入らず、着ていた衣類はぼろぼろ。

「何、あの人は？」「ものすごく臭いわね」

　みんなが和一を避けて通ります。

　それでも、和一は江ノ島の弁天さまが目の前にあることに勇気づけられて、急な石段を上りはじめました。

　やがて上の坊・中津宮というところにたどり着きました。

「ごめんください。突然ではありますが、断食修行のため参りました……」

　案内を願う和一は、破れ傘の貧しい身なりです。

「何？　その汚い姿で断食修行だと？　とんでもないことじゃ、すぐに島から追い出してしまえ」

　応対した修験者は、まるで野良犬を追い払うように、ものすごいけんまくで、取りつくしまもありません。

　──せっかく、訪ねてきたのに……──

　しかたなく和一は、さきほど上ってきた急な石段を、ころがるようにして下っていきました。草鞋はすりきれて裸足同然ですから、足の裏は傷だらけ。このままでは、島を出ることすらできません。

手をふりあげて追い返す修験者のけんまくに驚き、逃げ去る和一。

そのときです。和一の耳元で声がしました。

「どうなされました？」

「はっ？　どなたでしょうか？」

「これは、失礼いたしました。下の坊の恭順院と申します」

「ごらんのとおり盲目の身ですが、これからの鍼治療をどうしたらよいか、良い方法を弁天さまにうかがうために参りましたが、上の坊で叱られて逃げてきました」

「それは、それは、固い決心をなさっておられるのですね。上の坊では失礼なことを……」

「私は、何が何でも『新しい鍼術』の教えを乞うために、洞窟にこもって断食修行をする決心で参りました」

「よろしければ下の坊へお立ち寄りくださいませ。まずはお怪我の治療をなさってから、あなたさまの願いが、かなえられますようお手伝いをさせていただきます」

和一の耳にそっと手を寄せて、やさしく話す恭順院。

　捨てる神あれば拾う神ありのたとえではありませんが、まさに弁天さまのお導きなのでしょうか。和一は恭順院の厚意に甘えて、痛めた足の治療をしたあと、海岸沿いにある洞窟にこもって断食修行を始めました。

　これまでの旅で衰弱しきっている身体で断食をするのですから、命の危険を伴うこともあります。

　一日、二日目は雑念の悩み、三日、四日目は空腹とのたたかい、五日、六日目は生死の苦しみ、そして七日目をすぎるころ、不思議といろいろな悩みや迷い、苦しみから解き放たれたような気持ちになりました。

　八日目の朝、東の海が茜色に染まるころ、和一は心身ともに朦朧としてきました。

　――弁天さま、一週間断食を続けましたが、神さまからのお力やお告げをいただけませんでした。このまま一生他人さまの世話になって生きてゆくよりは、海に身を投げて死んだほうが楽になると思うようになりました。恭順院さまのお優しいお心遣いに何もお応えできないのが、本当に心苦しい……！

　和一は、心のなかで泣いて詫びるのでした。

洞窟にこもり、座禅に集中する和一。

悲しい気持ちでいっぱいの和一が、手探りで傍に置いてあった木の杖を握り、よろよろしながら洞窟を出て岩場を歩き始めた、そのときです。和一は、大きな石につまずいて倒れてしまいました。

「痛い！　何だ？」

　半ば朦朧としていた和一の足に何かがチクリと刺さったのです。あまりの痛さに和一はその場に座り込んでしまいました。手で触ると、一本の松葉が丸く筒状になった落ち葉にくるりと包まれた状態で皮膚に突き刺さっていました。和一は、すぐに、その細くとがった松葉を抜きましたが、次の瞬間、頭にひらめいたものがありました。

　─これだ！　細い「管」をつかい、そのなかに鍼を入れて用いれば、正確にツボを刺激できるはずだ。大発見だ、これこそ弁天さまのお告げだ！─

　希望が湧いてきた和一は、再び洞窟に戻り、弁天さまにお礼を申し上げました。

和一の手のひらには、一枚の葉にくるまれた一本の松葉が乗っている。その向こうに、弁財天の姿が浮かぶ。

　全身が衰弱して歩くこともおぼつかないほどでしたが、恭順院にこのことを知らせようと、和一はデコボコした岩場を必死になって歩きました。下の坊まで辿り着いたとき、突然、恭順院の声がしました。
「和一さん、お久しぶりです。毎日心配しておりましたよ」
「ああ、恭順院さまですね！　実は素晴らしい発見をいたしましたので、お知らせにうかがったのです」
「それは、それは、なんともうれしいことで……」

　和一は今にも倒れそうになりながらも、木の葉に包まれた松葉のことを、歓喜にむせびながら一気に説明しました。
「それにしても、あなたさまは断食で大変弱っておられます。よろしければ、ここで、しばらく静養なさったらいかがでしょうか」
　恭順院のお陰で、和一の健康は、みるみるうちに回復していきました。

恭順院のもとを訪ね、松葉を見せる和一。そのやせ細った姿に、断食修行の辛さがあらわれている。

元気になると、和一は、再び江戸の山瀬琢一のもとを訪ね、新しい鍼術の発見を師匠に報告しました。山瀬は大いに喜び、和一に診療所で新しい鍼術の稽古と鍼治療の修行を続けさせました。和一は盲人でも簡単で正確に針を打てるという全く新しい鍼術の工夫に没頭しました。人間の身体を本当に治療するとなると、まだまだ勉強し修業しなければならないと思うのでした。

　5年ほど経ったある日、山瀬は、和一をよんで言いました。
「和一よ、そなたがここに来たころは、まだなにもわからぬ少年だった。それが、いまでは立派にわしのかわりをつとめている」
「ありがとうございます。先生のおかげです」
「もう、わしが師匠として教えることもなくなった。ここらで、わしのもとをはなれて、もっと広く深く鍼医の道を学んでみないか」
　山瀬は、自分の師匠である入江良明を訪ねるよう、紹介状を書いて和一を京都に送り出すことにしました。真の鍼医になるためには、京で自分が学んだように、いろいろな技を学んでほしいという、師匠としての願いからでした。

　京への出発を前に、和一は江ノ島の恭順院のもとを訪ねました。
「いつも陰でお支えいただきありがとうございます。実は、『管鍼』を医術としてその治療に役立てるためには、できるだけ多くの先輩方を訪ね、学んでおくことが必要と思っています」
「どちらへいらっしゃるご予定ですか」
「京に、高名な師匠が何人もいらっしゃるのです」
「あなたさまがお考えになられたことですから、結構なことだと思います。ただ一つ、弁天さまのことだけは、お忘れにならないでくださいましね」
「当然でございます。毎朝必ず、江ノ島に向かって手を合わせることを、お約束いたします」
「私も、あなたさまのご無事と新しい鍼術が達成されるようお祈り申し上げます」
　恭順院から励ましの言葉をもらった和一は、これまでのお礼を申し上げ、身のまわりのわずかな荷物を背負い、杖を片手に京へと旅立ちました。

ひとりで黙々と鍼術の工夫に取り組む和一。

東海道を上り、小田原から関所を通るには、かごをつかいました。盲人とわかると、思いのほか、簡単に関所を通してくれました。

かごの乗り心地は決して良いとはいえませんが、和一が杖を頼りに歩くスピードに比べると大変な速さです。ところが、所持金が思ったよりも少なくなってきました。

三島でかごを降りた和一は、そこからは、もっぱら歩いて東海道を上ることに決めました。石ころだらけの道路に足をとられ、朝はいた草鞋は夕方になるとぼろぼろになって裸足と同じでした。でも、江戸から江ノ島への旅の経験から、和一は、はきかえ用の草鞋を何足か用意していたので助かりました。

長い道中、いろいろな人びとの親切にも出会いました。朝、目がさめると、必ず東のほうを向いて、旅の無事と弁天さまと恭順院への感謝をこめて、お祈りをすることを忘れませんでした。

朝、出発前に朝日の上る方向に向けてお祈りをする旅姿の和一。

しかし、困ったことも起きました。琵琶湖に近づいたころには、宿賃や食事代を節約したことがもとで、体力が急に衰えてきたのです。しかも野宿することが多くなり、着物もぼろぼろになり、見たところ物乞いのような姿です。
「すみません、旅の者ですが……」
　声をかけても、皆知らん顔をして通り過ぎます。
「まあ汚らしいこと」
「臭いし、おまけに目が見えないらしいよ」
　大きな声で言われて、和一の心は傷つくこともしばしばでした。それでも、自分が考えた管鍼の方法を深めたい一心で、京に向かって歩き続けました。

何処をどう歩いたかわかりません。人びとの話し声が聞こえてきました。どうやら、故郷に近い近江（現在の滋賀県）のあたりにたどり着いたようです。

どこからか、夕食の美味しそうな匂いが流れてきました。和一は、故郷の両親のことを思い出して、涙が止まりません。でも、家を出るときの決心を思えば、帰るわけにはいきません。

どうにか京の都にたどり着くと、和一は、ついに力つきて倒れてしまいました。

「どうした、どうした。誰だ！」

「なんじゃ、行き倒れかい。汚らしい」

「この人、目が見えんらしい。杖をついてよろよろしながら歩いていやはったそうな」

大勢の人が集まってはいるのですが、ただ遠巻きにして見ているだけでした。

その時です。近くの立派な家から数人の男女が駆けつけてきました。

「どうなさいました？」

「人が突然倒れはったんや」

「えっ、それは大変や、早う師匠を呼んで！」

若い男があわてて家に戻ると、まもなくいかにも風格のある品の良い男性が現れて、倒れた和一の腕をとり、脈を確かめました。

「脈がかなり弱いですね。医療箱をください」

箱のなかから、鍼を取り出すと、手早く鍼を打ち始めました。

野次馬たちは、おそるおそるその様子を眺めていましたが、やがて、

「あっ、生き返った！　動いた！」

と驚きの声をあげました。

「意識はもどりましたが、たいへん弱っていますから、しばらくの間、うちでお世話しましょう」

実は、この人物が、京の地で有名な鍼医の入江豊明だったのです。

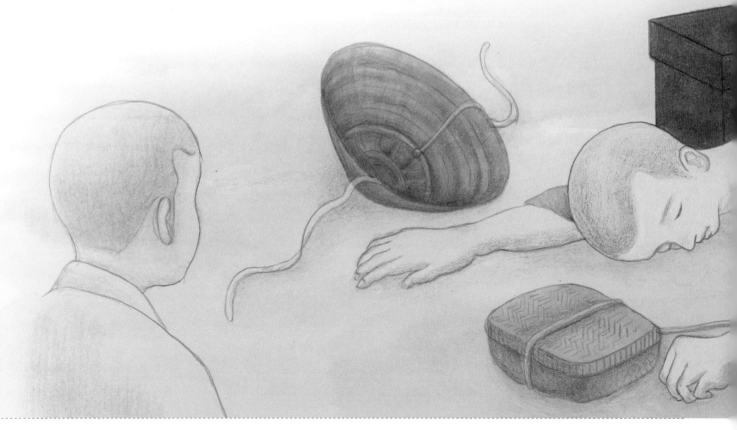

旅姿のまま道に倒れた和一に鍼治療をする男性。まわりでは、人びとが見守っている。

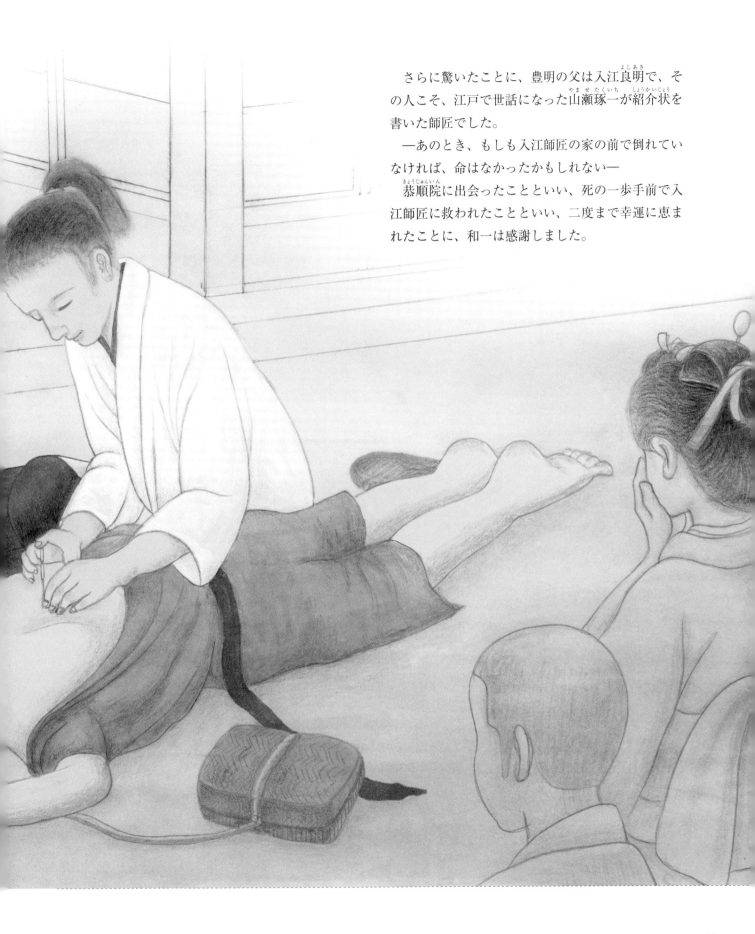

　さらに驚いたことに、豊明の父は入江良明で、その人こそ、江戸で世話になった山瀬琢一が紹介状を書いた師匠でした。

　――あのとき、もしも入江師匠の家の前で倒れていなければ、命はなかったかもしれない――

　恭順院に出会ったことといい、死の一歩手前で入江師匠に救われたことといい、二度まで幸運に恵まれたことに、和一は感謝しました。

入江治療所の人びとの親切な看病のおかげで、和一は日ましに、日ごとに元気になっていきました。時が経つにつれて、入江師匠が立派な人物で、多くの人から尊敬されていることもわかってきました。弟子たちが自主的に医学の勉強をしていることにも気がつきました。

　毎晩、患者さんが帰ったあと、弟子たちが大部屋に集まり、師匠から教えられたことを3回くりかえして覚えていくのです。和一でも、同じことを3回くりかえすと、不思議と覚えられます。こうした弟子たちの真剣な態度に、和一は、これまでの自分の甘さを反省しました。

　和一の体調が回復すると、入江師匠から、
「きみは今後、どうするつもりかね」
　と声をかけられ、和一は自分の気持ちを素直に話しました。
「師匠、誠に勝手なお願いではありますが、内弟子にしていただけませんでしょうか」

「おお、そのような心境にいたったのか。だが、きみは新しい鍼の技術を工夫中と聞いている。今回、そなたが私どもの治療所で学びたいという一番の動機は何かね？」
「はい、師匠のお宅でお世話になっておりますあいだに、二つのことを強く感じました。

　一つは、師匠が人の身体の成り立ちを確かめた上で、治療なさっておられること。二つ目は、内弟子の方々がむずかしい医学書を完全に理解した上で、なおも日々深く学んでおられることです」
「よし、わかった。特別扱いはしないぞ。目が見えないということを忘れてやれるかね」
「はい」
「江戸の山瀬琢一師匠のところより数倍は厳しいですぞ。この仕事は、人の命をあずかる仕事だから、まず人格を磨いて、だれにも負けない治療の技術を身につけるように努力しなさい」

諭している入江師匠と、それに真摯に向き合う和一のシルエット。

　山瀬師匠のところでは毎朝5時起きでした。しかし、入江塾では弟子たちは5時前には、それぞれの仕事にとりかかれるように準備ができていました。庭掃除、屋内の清掃、朝の食事づくりなど、役割を分担しながら、皆黙々と働いています。

　和一には廊下の雑巾がけが割り当てられました。広い家のことですから、思ったよりたいへんです。やがて、障子やふすま、お手洗いまで、和一がするよう言われました。毎日、2時間以上もかけての掃除の後、先輩から掃除のできばえを見てもらいます。

　1日の仕事が終わり、夕食の後片付けが済むと、ほんのわずかな時間をさいて、その日の患者さんの病気や治療法について、皆で熱心に話し合います。

　——毎日毎日が真剣勝負なのだなぁ……——

　和一は感心するばかりでしたが、その和一も、今では、これまであまり覚えられなかったことも覚えられるようになりました。

車座になって熱心に話し合う塾生たち。

師匠やその弟子たちは、和一のために時間をさいて、手を添えて熱心に教えてくれました。しかし、どれほどやっても、和一は上手に鍼を打つことができません。

兄弟子たちが、患者役になって鍼を打たせてくれるのですが、「痛い」といわれるだけで、治療効果が上がりません。

「むずかしいのは皆同じ。入江師匠でさえ、自分の思いどおりに鍼を打てるようになるのに、何十年もかかったとおっしゃっていましたよ」

自信をなくしていく和一に、兄弟子たちは優しく声をかけてくれました。

「鍼治療の道は、遠くに見える小さな灯火を頼りに、山道をコツコツと歩んでいくようなものなのです」

「せっかく、ここで修業しているのだから、師匠が治療をなさっておられるとき、近くで仕事をしながら患者さんに話していらっしゃる言葉をよく聞いてみなはれ。これは弟子の特権やからね」

和一は、兄弟子たちの言葉に感謝し、さっそく従うことにしました。

師匠の治療室は一枚の戸でしきられた簡素な部屋でしたが、治療中は物音一つしない静かさです。師匠が、小さな声でときどき患者さんに話しかける様子からも、緊張感が伝わってきます。やがて治療が終わると、患者さんが明るい声でお礼を言うのが聞こえます。その時、師匠が

「お大事になさってください。ありがとうございました」

とお礼を言っているのを聞き、和一はびっくりしました。

—そうか、この仕事は、治療してあげるという気持ちではいけないのだ—

和一は治療の知識や技術の他に、師匠の人間的な素晴らしさにふれて大きく成長するのでした。

ある日、和一は師匠から、回復が近い患者さんの治療をまかされました。

「痛い痛い」

やはりうまくいきません。

「失礼いたしました。私の責任でございます。お許しください。これからは、私が治療させていただきます」

師匠からの言葉に、患者さんも納得しました。

治療室で使われている鍼が並んでいる。

　その晩、すべての患者さんが帰ったあとで、師匠は和一を自分の部屋に呼びました。
「お前がここへきて７年。入江流の鍼術の技と理論をきびしく教えてきたが、理論の勉強は順調に進んだようでも、鍼術の技術だけは、どうしてもその奥義を究めることがむずかしいようだ。お前の熱意はわかるが、入江流の治療法は、全盲のお前には向かないように思う。盲人の身であるお前にふさわしい鍼術の技をみがくためには、まだまだ工夫が必要だ。この際、お前が取り組んでいる新しい鍼術の技をみがくために、京にいるほかの師匠に師事してみてはどうかね」
　入江師匠の口からは破門という言葉は出ませんでした。和一には師匠が言いたいことの意味が理解で

きました。
「先生のおしゃるとおりにいたします」
　翌朝、和一は命の恩人であり、入江流鍼術の奥義のほか多くのことを教えてくれた師匠に感謝の言葉を述べ、その教えに十分答えることができなかったことを詫びました。そのうえで、京の地でほかの先輩師匠にお願いして医術の勉強を続ける決意を伝えました。
「それは、結構なことだ。お前に学ぼうとする意思があれば、必ずや、みなに通じるであろう。お前のことは決して忘れることはない。例の管鍼術で成功することを祈っている」
　入江師匠の人物の大きさに感謝して、和一は門を出ました。

玄関で、入江師匠にお別れのあいさつをする和一。

和一は、京の御園意斎など、鍼博士とよばれている有名な実力者に次つぎに弟子入りして、多くの知識とそれぞれの師匠の鍼治療について学びました。

　どうにか、自分流の鍼治療ができるようになったときには、和一は40代になっていました。

　—さあ、いよいよ江戸に戻って自分の診療所を開こう—

　和一は、江戸城に近い麹町（現在の東京都千代田区）に診療所を開き、私邸内に杉山塾という私塾を開くことにしました。まずは、以前お世話になった山瀬琢一師匠宅への挨拶です。

「お前はきっと何かをやれる人物だと思っていたよ……」

　琢一はわがことのように喜び、大きな心で和一の門出を祝福してくれました。

　それまでの鍼治療法は、中国から伝わった太い鍼を手で刺すものでしたから、患者さんにとっては痛いものでした。しかし、和一が考案した管鍼術は痛みが非常に少なく、かつ良いものでした。

「麹町の鍼治療は実によく効くよ。これまでとちがって痛くないんだよ」

　患者さんからの評判が評判を呼んで、管鍼術はあっという間にその名が江戸だけではなく、上方（関西地方）にまで知れわたっていきました。

　和一は、まわりの言葉にも決しておごることがありませんでした。

「まだまだ勉強中」

　といって、わずかな時間を惜しんでは、京で得た知識を元に、管鍼術の完成に日夜うちこみました。

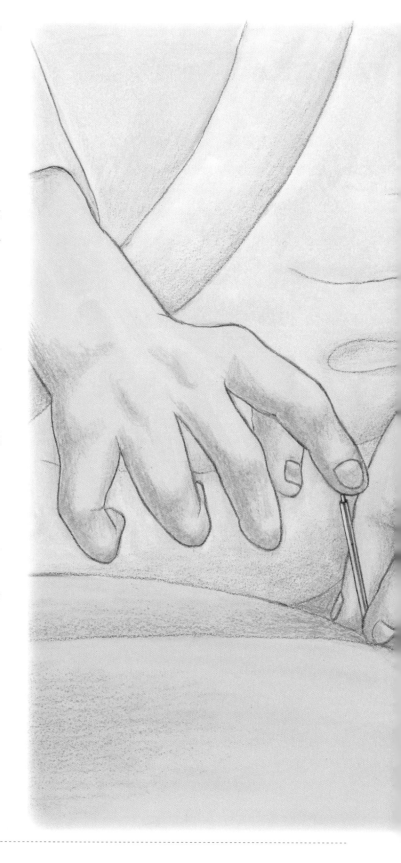

管鍼術で治療をする和一。管に通した鍼を患者の身体に刺しているようす。

24

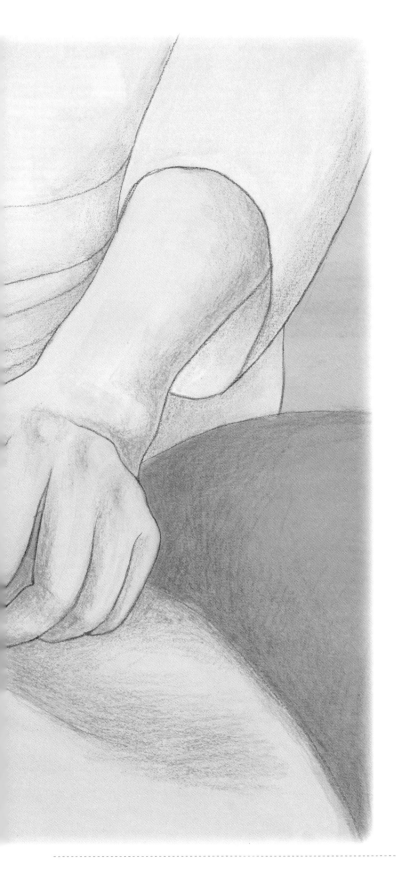

　和一が考案した管鍼術は、細い鍼を管に入れ、施術（せじゅつ）するものでした。鍼を通す管としてつかう細い竹はすぐに手に入りますが、枯（か）れたり折れたりします。和一はあれやこれや考えた挙句（あげく）に、金属製の細い管が最適だと思いつきました。しかし、それを完成させるためには、金属を筒型（つつがた）に細く丸める高度な技術をもった職人さんの協力が必要でした。

　次の課題は鍼のかたちです。当時の鍼は「捻（ひね）り鍼（はり）」といって直接に皮膚（ひふ）に刺すため、刺すときに曲がらないように根本（ねもと）が太いものでした。管に通すためには、松葉のように根本から鍼先まで同じ太さでなければなりません。松葉のような新しい鍼の開発が必要です。

　さらに、管に通した鍼を身体に刺すための工夫（くふう）も必要でした。これには日本で開発されていた鍼の頭を小槌（こづち）でたたいて入れる「打鍼法（だしんほう）」がヒントになりました。管からわずかに出ている鍼の頭を小槌の代わりに指先で軽くたたいて入れる「切皮法（せっぴほう）」というテクニックを考案し、無痛で刺せるようになりました。

　こうして開発された「管鍼術」は、細い鍼を、痛むことなく目的のツボに正確に刺し入れることができるという点で、盲人（もうじん）だけでなく晴眼者（せいがんしゃ）（目の見える人）の鍼医からも注目されるようになっていきました。

　そればかりではありません。和一は治療効果を高めるために工夫をし、100種類にも及（およ）ぶ管鍼の刺し入れ法を編み出し、完成させました。

　幸いなことに、このころには、出雲国（いずものくに）（現在の島根県（しまねけん））の石見銀山（いわみぎんざん）や越後（えちご）の国（現在の新潟県（にいがたけん））の佐渡金山（さどきんざん）から、かなりの量の金や銀がとれました。鍼治療に必要な金や銀が手に入りやすいこともあって、次々と新しい良い鍼管（しんかん）（鍼の管）や鍼ができるようになり、その名声は日本国中に広がっていきました。

ここで、「当道座」とよばれる盲人の互助団体についてふれておきましょう。

江戸時代、盲人は「当道座」という組合の一員になるのが一般的でした。検校、別当、勾当、座頭などという位をつくり、これをお金で買うようにして、集まったお金を位に応じて分配するという、いまでいう年金制度のようなものです。

和一は、1670（寛文10）年正月元旦、61歳で「検校」の地位につきました。検校という地位は、73段階に分かれている階級での最高位です。当道座の大部分の人たちは、箏や三味線、琵琶など音曲の先生で占められていました。鍼医で検校となったのは、杉山流の「管鍼術」による鍼治療が高い評価を受けていることと、和一の誠実温厚な人がらが認められたからでした。

和一の評価は高まり、ついには幕府の将軍からも強い関心を持たれるようになりました。

検校の姿をして座っている和一。

1680（延宝8）年のことでした。幕府のお抱え医師である井上玄徹から和一にお呼びがかかりました。四代将軍徳川家綱の病状が思わしくないというのです。家綱の病状は思いのほか悪く、和一も戸惑いました。一心に治療にあたった結果、一時的には痛みも薄れ、お付きの人たちも喜びました。しかし検校である和一には、将軍の病気が重大な状況であることがわかっていました。

「この度、お声をおかけくださり感激しておりま

す。鍼をしますと、一時的には血液の循環がよくなりますので、ご病状が良くなられたようにお見受けなさるでしょうが、ここ、一ヶ月が峠のようでございます」

お付きの人たちは一瞬、驚きましたが、不幸にも和一の診断は間違いではありませんでした。それから一ヶ月後の5月8日、治療のかいもなく、将軍家綱は、40歳という短い生涯を終えました。

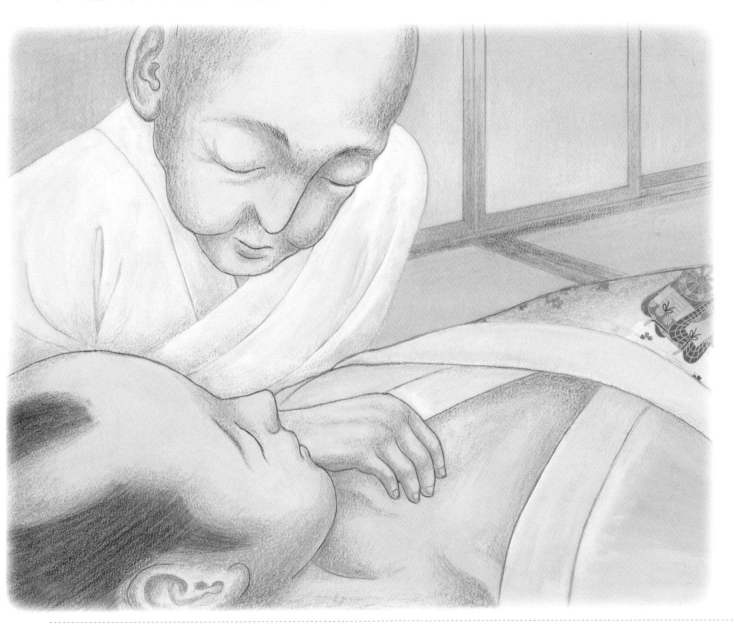

徳川家綱の身体に手を置き、診断する和一。

一方、杉山塾は、診療所として人気をよんでいました。朝、玄関を開けると、そこには何人もの患者さんが列をなしています。

　だれか手伝ってくれる人を探さないと、全盲の和一だけではやりくりするのがむずかしくなってきました。そこで、家事一切をしてもらえるお手伝いさんを探してもらうことにしました。さっそく、紹介されたのが、セツという女性です。若くて聡明で気立ての良い彼女は、杉山塾ではたらくことになりました。

　杉山塾の一日は、朝5時からはじまります。セツは和一の身の回りの世話をしたあと、掃除、洗濯、炊事、治療室の準備にいたるまで、すべてにわたって実によく働きました。杉山塾は大繁盛で、セツは患者さんにとってもなくてはならない人になっていました。
「セツよ、ありがとう。あなたのような働き者は珍しいよ。良い人に出会えてうれしいよ」
「いえいえ、まだまだでございます。なんなりとお申し付けくださいまし」
「ありがとう。実は一つお願いがあるのじゃ。毎月一回、江ノ島まで連れて行ってほしいのじゃ」
「お師匠さまのお申し付けでしたら、喜んでお供させていただきます」

掃除、洗濯、料理、配膳など、こまめに働くセツのようす。

　以後、和一は、どんなに仕事が忙し
くても、毎月江ノ島を訪ね、弁天さま
に「管鍼」の開発のお礼と感謝の月参
りを欠かすことなく続けました。

　初めてセツを連れて江ノ島に行った
ときは、弁天さまにお参りしたあと、
セツに管鍼術を思いついた地である洞
窟を教えました。

「セツや、ここが、わしの生涯の原点
なのだ」

「前からお話では伺っておりました
が、今、改めてお師匠さまの深い思い
がわかりました」

　いつまでも岩場にたたずみ、一心不
乱に何かを口ずさんでいる和一の姿
に、セツは不思議な感動を覚え、自分
の生涯を和一のために捧げようと決心
するのでした。

　その帰り道、和一は恭順院を訪ねま
した。毎朝、弁天さまにお祈りしてい
ること、恭順院の支えがどんなに大き
かったかを感謝し、さらに、いま傍
にいるセツという素晴らしい理解者の
おかげで杉山塾が大変助かっているこ
となどを話しました。

　その後、弁天さまに特別な思い入れ
のある和一は、藤沢の宿から江ノ島へ
向かう江ノ島道に48本の"道標"を建て
ました。一般の参拝者はもちろん、盲
人でも弁天さまにお参りしやすいよう
にしたのです。また、海岸岬には漁師
たちの海難事故を防ぐため、竜灯（常
夜灯）も建てました。

　1682（天和2）年、72歳の和一は、目に障害のある人のために「鍼治講習所」という教育の場（学校）を開設しました。鍼治講習所では和一の考案した「管鍼術」をはじめ、「鍼灸・あん摩」という医療の学問と技術を教えました。これは、後の「盲学校・鍼灸・あん摩師養成所」のさきがけです。フランス人のバランタン・アユイがヨーロッパで盲人教育所を始めたのが1784年ですから、それよりも100年も前にこのような教育の場ができていたことは、世界に誇れることです。

　この講習所は、一番弟子の三嶋安一らによって、江戸の四街道の出口である品川、新宿、板橋、千住の4箇所をはじめ全国45箇所に開かれました。こ

れらが、現在の全国各県の盲学校の基礎となっています。

　盲人教育の場所が決まると、和一は指導のための教科書の作成に取りかかりました。

　管鍼術の理論と技法を正確に後の世まで伝えるためには、今までのような口伝えで教えていくのではなく、学問として通用する教科書をつくり、教育することが何より重要だと和一は考えました。それで、自分でつくった指導書をもとに、その治療法を弟子たちに伝えたいという大きな夢を持ったのです。めざしたのは、目の不自由な人が鍼医として自立していくための職業教育の実現でした。

「鍼治講習所」と看板がつけられた一軒家の入口。

和一は盲人ですから、何かを文字にして残すことはできません（フランスのルイ・ブライユによって、点字という素晴らしい方法が考え出されたのは、その後150年経ってからです）。

　まず最初は、セツに口述筆記を頼みました。ところが鍼術の専門用語が多く、セツには負担が大きいことがわかりました。そこで、友人、知人に頼んで適当な人を探してもらうのですが、江戸広しといえども、なかなか見つかりません。鍼独自のむずかしい用語を漢字で正確に書き残すには、医学の専門知識が必要です。和一自身、言葉は知っていても、「どういう漢字ですか」と聞かれると困ってしまいます。専門の鍼医書をつくることのむずかしさを改めて感じて戸惑うばかりでした。

　それでも、和一はくじけません。患者の治療を終えたあと、毎晩遅くまで、指導書をつくる努力を続けました。

　いろいろな考えが思い浮かぶので、その考えをとにかく書き残しておくことから始めよう。そう考えると気持ちも楽になり、適任者が見つかるまでは、セツに書き留めておいてもらえばよいと、和一は考えました。

　さすがにセツは、無理ですと言って断りましたが、和一はねばります。

「ひらがなで、わしの思いついたことを書き留めてくれればよい。それで十分なのだ」

　師匠の熱心な頼みに、セツはついに理解を示しました。

　翌日からは、一日の仕事が終わると口述筆記です。和一の頭のなかも整理されていくのでしょう。次々と良い考えが浮かんできます。

「セツが協力してくれるおかげで本当に助かる。この世の中、ことばも大切じゃが、文書で記録しておかないと消えてなくなってしまうのじゃ」

「お師匠さま、本当にそのとおりでございます。こんな私でも多少なりともお役に立てれば、うれしい限りでございます」

和一の話を聞きながら、一語ずつ筆で書き留めるセツ。

杉山塾は、毎日多くの患者さんでいっぱいでした。それでも和一は、その忙しさのなかで、黙々と管鍼術の完成と指導書づくりに心をくだきました。後に『杉山流三部書』*とよばれる医書の草稿ができあがったのも、このころです。

鍼治講習所（学問所）は幕府に公認され、指導書ができあがると、優秀な人たちがたくさん集まってきました。今までは、師匠が弟子に伝えるには記憶に頼るといった方法だけでした。しかし鍼治講習所では指導書があるのです。和一の進んだ考え方に、みな感心するのでした。

検校という立場になり、和一は、今までの鍼治療のほかに幕府との話しあいなどで忙しい毎日が続きました。しかし多忙ななか、和一は次の仕事として、自分と同じ盲人のなかから優秀な弟子を育てることを考えていました。当時、盲人の多くは琴や三味線で生活する人や、あん摩だけの道を選ぶ人が多く、技術的にむずかしい鍼治療の道を選ぶ人はあまりいなかったのです。

なかには杉山塾が繁盛していると聞いて、「鍼治療のほうが繁盛する」といった安易な気持ちで弟子入りを希望してくる人がいます。そういう人が訪れ

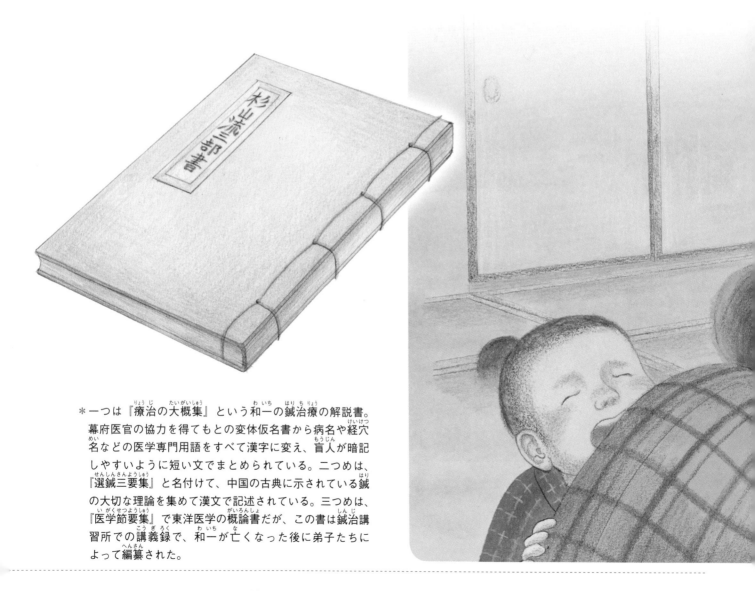

＊一つは『療治の大概集』という和一の鍼治療の解説書。幕府医官の協力を得てもとの変体仮名書から病名や経穴名などの医学専門用語をすべて漢字に変え、盲人が暗記しやすいように短い文でまとめられている。二つめは、『選鍼三要集』と名付けて、中国の古典に示されている鍼の大切な理論を集めて漢文で記述されている。三つめは、『医学節要集』で東洋医学の概論書だが、この書は鍼治講習所での講義録で、和一が亡くなった後に弟子たちによって編纂された。

指導書として、ひも閉じ製本された「杉山流三部書」。

ると、和一は強い口調でたしなめます。

「わざわざ遠くから江戸へ来られたようだが、わしは金儲けをさせるために弟子を求めているのではない。『管鍼術』は生涯をかけて技術を磨いて病に苦しむ人を救うものだ」

こんなこともありました。生まれつき目が見えない息子を連れてきた父親が、弟子入りを和一に頼んだときのこと。

「寄付をさせていただきますので……」

と言ったとたん、

「わしは金がほしくてこの仕事をしているのではない！　そのような不純な動機で『鍼術』をやろうというのはもってのほかじゃ、帰りなさい！」

普段は温厚な和一が、烈火のごとく怒って追い返してしまいました。

和一は弟子を選ぶのに、理解力や技術以上に人柄を重んじました。多くの入門希望者のなかから選ばれたのは、目が見えなくても優秀な人たちでした。やがて、この講習所から優秀な門弟が次々に独立していき、地方の藩でも活躍するようになりました。

寄付を理由に息子の弟子入りを頼む父親に、こぶしを振り上げ、はげしく怒る和一。

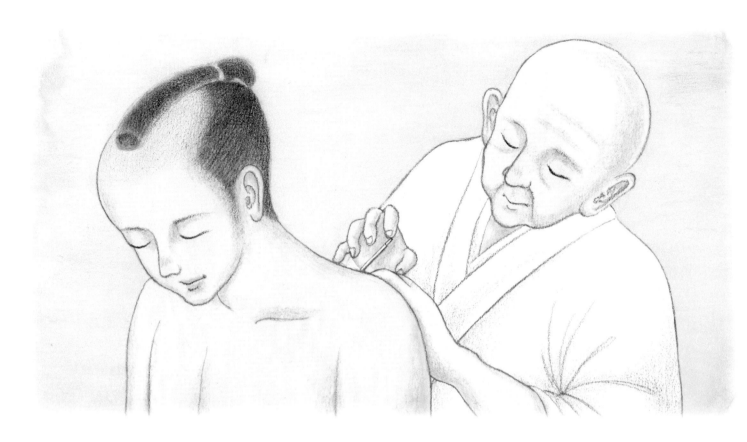

ところで、四代将軍・家綱が亡くなった後、異母弟の綱吉が、わずか35歳で第5代将軍となりました。綱吉は学問に興味を示し、勉強熱心で、役人の不正を許さないという人でしたが、反面、小心なところがありました。

あるとき、綱吉が将軍になったのを不満に思ったものが、綱吉の家来を刺すという事件があり、そのことで綱吉は精神的に不安定になってしまいました。そのころの人は、いまでいうノイローゼのことを「ぶらぶら病」と呼んでいました。綱吉が、いわゆるぶらぶら病だということに気づいたお付きのものが、和一に治療を頼みました。

最初は不機嫌そうだった綱吉でしたが、和一が鍼治療を始めると、いつしか気持ちよさそうに寝入ってしまいました。治療が終わり、お付きの者が静かに声をかけると、綱吉の顔から先程までのピリピリした神経質な表情が消えて、別人のような穏やかな顔つきに変わっています。

「あと数回続けますと、快方に向かうと思われますが……」

まもなく綱吉のぶらぶら病は、完治しました。綱吉はたいへん喜び、和一に多額の褒美とともに、お抱え侍医として月俸（手当）をあたえ、さらに大手町に屋敷まで用意しました。和一がどんなに丁重にあつかわれたかがわかります。

和一はこうした将軍家の厚意に思い上がることなく、将軍家の幸せを祈るという純粋な気持ちから、毎月、江ノ島の下の坊を訪れて密かに厄除け祈願を続けていました。このことが、やがて幕府の役人の知るところとなり、和一の誠実な人柄にたいして、関係者一同涙を流して感謝しました。

その功績が高く評価され、和一は御家人から旗本に昇格しただけではなく、1689（元禄2）年、小川町に500坪（現在の1600平方メートル）あまりの敷地を賜りました。和一が80歳をすぎると、将軍は年老いた和一を労って、大奥までかごで出入りすることを許すまでになりました。

徳川綱吉に鍼治療をする和一。

81歳のとき、和一は重い病気にかかりました。心配したセツは和一の病状が、やや落ち着いたのを見計らい、江ノ島の弁天さまにかけつけ祈願しました。
「弁天さま、どうか検校さまの病を治してくださいませ。もし命を助けてくださいましたら、我が身をお捧げいたします」
　セツの強い祈りが通じたのでしょうか。和一は奇跡的に回復しました。
　このことを誰よりも喜んだのはセツでしたが、ま

もなくセツは江ノ島の海に身を投げ、一生を終えたのです。弁天さまとの約束をはたすためでしょう。
　セツの突然の死を知った和一の気持ちは、どのようなものだったのでしょうか。セツの生命をかけた働きに感謝するものの、あまりの悲しい別れに何も手につきません。
「わしがこの世を去ったときには、必ずセツの墓もわしの側に建ててほしい。忘れるではないぞ」
　セツへの想いを胸に、和一は、弟子に頼みました。

和一のまぶたの向こうに、手を合わせて穏やかな顔で祈るセツがいる。

その翌年1692（元禄5）年、将軍綱吉の命により、和一は、82歳にして、「当道座」の最高位である関東総検校に任ぜられました。セツが生きていれば、どんなに喜んだことでしょう。

総検校の責任をはたすために、和一は、当道座の大々的な組織改革に取り組みました。乱れていた式目（当時の規則）を正して鍼灸・あん摩療法の道だけではなく、箏曲や琵琶などの音楽の道や金融業の仕事についても整えて、盲人の生業（職業）の道をも確かなものとしたのです。

ある日、将軍綱吉は和一を呼んで言いました。
「爺や、そなたは、今でも毎月江ノ島の弁財天にお参りしているようだが」
「はい、歩けるうちは生涯続けるつもりでおりましたが、最近は年のせいでしょうか、かなりきつく感じるようになりました」
「総検校の誠を尽くす信念は立派だが、この際、別の方法を考えたらいかがかな」
「別の方法と申しますと？」
「いや、このようなものを用意したのじゃ」

将軍はお付きの者に言って、三尺（約1メートル）ほどの立派な桐の箱を和一の前に持ってこさせました。
「爺や、これは、余が心をこめてつくらせたものじゃ。まずは、ようく触ってみてほしい」

和一は包まれていた白い布の上から、ていねいに触って、すぐにわかったようです。
「立派なお像のように思われますが……」
「さすが、鋭い感覚じゃ。これは『黄金の弁天像』じゃ。これからは江ノ島に通う代わりに、近くの寺社にこれを納めて祈願するがよかろう」

そして、総検校に問いかけました。
「これまで余に尽くしてくれたことに褒美をとらせよう。今、いちばん欲しいものをなんなりと申せ」

こうした心配りに、ただ感激し恐縮していた和一は、固く辞退しましたが、将軍に、
「なにか一つくらいはあるだろう」
と言われると、ようやく重い口を開きました。

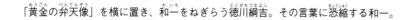

「黄金の弁天像」を横に置き、和一をねぎらう徳川綱吉。その言葉に恐縮する和一。

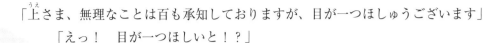

「上さま、無理なことは百も承知しておりますが、目が一つほしゅうございます」

「えっ！　目が一つほしいと！？」

さすがに将軍も困られたようでしたが、数日後、返事が届きました。

「望みにより一つ目を与えよう」

といい、「一ツ目（現在の墨田区千歳）」という地名のおよそ三千坪（1万平方メートル）の土地を和一に与えたのです。

和一は、この将軍のとんちに感激して、

「上さまからいろいろご配慮いただき、感謝しております。この土地を自分だけのためではなく、世間の人びとのためにも使いたいと考えております」

と申し上げると、将軍はこう答えました。

「実は総検校に『黄金の弁天像』を送ったのは、一つ目の敷地内に弁天社を建てて、そこに弁天像を奉納すれば、毎日祈願できると考えたからなのじゃ」

やがて「黄金の弁天像」を収める「弁天社」の建設が始まりました。

「私は盲人で細かなことまで申せませんが、弁天さまに喜んでいただけるような立派なお社にしてください」

和一の言葉に大工の棟梁も心を打たれて、真心をこめて建設にあたりました。弁天社は豪華というより気品を感じさせるものでした。

黄金の弁天像の噂は江戸じゅうに広まって、毎日多くの人が祈願に訪れるようになりました。駒形から船に乗って参詣する人も増え、江戸の「一つ目弁天」として名所になり、一ツ目の地は惣録屋敷ともいわれて、100年余りのあいだ、盲人をまとめる役所と鍼治講習所が置かれました。

将軍綱吉は天下の悪法といわれた「生類憐れみの令」を出して、特に犬を厚く保護したことで知られています。しかし、その内容は、幼児や高齢者、障害者など社会的な弱者も保護の対象となっていました。杉山和一との出会いがきっかけとなって、盲人の社会的地位向上のために、大きな働きをしたことは意外と知られていないのです。

　1694（元禄7）年、和一は84歳を迎えましたが、鍼治療に対する研究心は衰えることはありませんでした。将軍の脈をとり、鍼治療をすることと、弁天さまへのお参りが日課でした。

　将軍から特別に許可された赤い裃姿をまとった和一が一心に祈願している姿は、その道を究めた人の風格と神仏を思わせるような存在感を周囲に示しました。そしてわずかな時間も惜しんで研鑽をつづける和一に感心し、だれもが口ぐちにその治療効果を高く評価するのでした。

　生まれつき身体が弱かった将軍は、ぶらぶら病が治ってからも和一の人物と治療技術に大きな信頼を寄せていました。しかし、和一も寄る年波には勝てず、まるで大木が朽ちていくように、5月20日、眠るように84年の天寿を全うしました。

　葬儀は立川の弥勒寺で弟子らに見守られておごそかに行われました。そしてここにお墓が建てられ、現在、治療鍼に感謝する「鍼供養塔」と並んで東京都の史跡にもなっています。

　翌年の1695（元禄8）年には、江ノ島辺津宮の下にお墓が建てられて納骨されましたが、その傍には和一の遺言どおり、セツのお墓も建てられました。

　その後、時代が変わって、和一に与えられた土地は明治政府によって没収、和一の私邸内から移ってきた鍼治講習所も閉鎖されましたが、弁天社だけは江島杉山神社として、目の不自由な人や鍼治療の関係者によって今日も大切に守られています。

　2016年、生誕400年を機に、和一を尊敬する人たちの"心の拠りどころ"として、神社の一角に和一ゆかりの資料を集めた記念館が建てられました。なかには「杉山鍼按治療所」が併設され、視覚障害者と晴眼者の鍼灸師が当番制で施術をおこなっています。

　和一が苦労して創案した「管鍼術」は、その優れた特色から一般の人たちにも受けいれられていきました。いまでは鍼灸師は、国家資格をもつ医療職です。盲人の職業の道を確かなものにしたいという和一の夢は、現実となったのです。

いまも東京の墨田区千歳にある「江島杉山神社」。

読者のみなさまへ

　本書は、今から400年ほど前の江戸時代に、現在の三重県津市で誕生した視覚障害のある偉人の一生をもとにつくられた絵本です。その人の名は「杉山和一」。鍼灸の神様とも呼ばれ、総検校まで昇り詰めただけでなく、同じ視覚障害者のための施策もおこなった人です。その働きは、世界的にも評価される功績であることが絵本からも読み取れます。

　和一は、幾多の難題にもめげず、努力と神仏の力を忘れずに管鍼術を考案し、その技術を普及させました。そのことを、鍼灸界で知らない人はいないでしょう。また、「杉山流鍼治導引稽古所」として、視覚障害者のための教育施設を最初に開校したのも和一でした。稽古所からは多くの有能な人材が育っていきました。江戸時代に視覚障害者の鍼灸・あん摩の学校を設立させたことは、明治時代の盲学校設立の礎となりました。世界でも稀なる視覚障害者の自立のための職業教育へと繋がっているのです。

　手先が器用でなくても地道な努力により技術改良を行い、容易に鍼をさせるよう改良した手腕は、医書「杉山流三部書」として受け継がれました。残された書物は教育のための財産となります。

　平均寿命の短い時代に、60歳を過ぎて検校へ昇進し、鍼師としての名声を残し、その後は関東総検校にも任命され盲人を統括する立場につきました。まさに典型的な大器晩成型の人物です。将軍綱吉に寵愛を受け、本所一つ目にある土地を与えられ、現在その一角が東京両国に現存する江島杉山神社となって残っています。

　良き人柄として想いうかべるのが、杉山和一が詠んだ和歌の一首です。「呼ばばゆけ　呼ばずば見舞へ　怠らず　折ふしごとに　おとづれをせよ」。この和歌に、医療人としての生き様のすべてが集約されているように思えます。

　絵本の作成は、文では今村鎭夫氏の巧みな文体により、杉山和一の一生をうまくまとめていただきました。吉澤みかさんの描いた絵は、江戸期の情景が生き生きと描かれています。

　本書の発行にあたり、小学館、一般財団法人日本児童教育振興財団より、ご支援を賜わりましたことに厚く御礼申し上げます。また、この絵本の製作に関わっていただいた全ての方々に感謝申し上げます。

2022年12月
社会福祉法人　桜雲会　理事長　一幡良利

文／今村鎭夫
1933年10月18日横浜生まれ。横浜訓盲学院で教鞭をとる父親のもと、幼少期のころは訓盲院でよく遊ぶ。大学卒業後、横浜訓盲学院の教師、横浜訓盲院の指導員となる。のちに同施設長。福祉系短大の非常勤講師も務めた。現在、横浜訓盲院評議員。

絵／吉澤みか
1963年京都府生まれ。日本画家。京都精華大学美術学部造形学科日本画専攻卒業。京都市立芸術大学美術学部大学院修了。京都美術展（奨励賞受賞）、京展はか入選多数。大人も読める絵本『ざっそう weeds』『駅のピアノ　故国への想い』（ともに今人舎）の絵を担当。

英訳／ノビ・キーリ（Nobby Kealey）
1957年イギリス・マンチェスター生まれ。シェフィールド大学にて日本語を専攻。来日後はカメラマンとして活躍する一方、英語教師のほか、数々のテレビCMに出演。松蔭学園イングリッシュ・スクール校長。

監修／社会福祉法人　桜雲会
1892年、東京盲啞学校（現在の筑波大学附属視覚特別支援学校）の生徒の同窓会として発足。1930年に最初の鍼按科教科書を出版。以後、医学専門書を中心に点字図書や録音図書、拡大図書の製作・販売をおこなう。

本文監修／大浦慈観

協力／杉山検校遺徳顕彰会

編集・デザイン・DTP制作／
　株式会社 今人舎（二宮祐子／矢野瑛子）

おもな参考資料
・『杉山和一～目の見えない人たちを救った偉人～』
　（財団法人杉山検校遺徳顕彰会　発行）

この図書は、一般財団法人日本児童教育振興財団の助成により制作いたしました。

世界に誇れる盲偉人 杉山和一　―江戸期に視覚障害者の職業教育施設を開校

2023年1月15日 第1刷発行
2023年4月15日 第2刷発行

NDC289

文	今村鎭夫
絵	吉澤みか
発行者	一幡良利
発行所	社会福祉法人桜雲会

〒169-0075 東京都新宿区高田馬場4-11-14-102
電話　03-5337-7866
http://ounkai.jp

印刷・製本　瞬報社写真印刷株式会社

©Shizuo Imamura, Mika Yoshizawa 2023, Printed in Japan, Published by Ounkai
ISBN978-4-904611-90-6　C0723

48P　210×260mm

Sugiyama Waichi, A Blind Leader Acclaimed By The World.

~The Opening Of Vocational Training Facilities For The Visually-Impaired In The Edo Period~

P1

In 1610, at the beginning of the Edo era (Keicho 15), an intelligent-looking child was born into the household of Sugiyama Gonuemon Shigemasa, a samurai in the service of Todo Takatora, lord of the castle in Anotsu in the province of Ise (present day Tsu City, Mie Prefecture).

The boy was named Yasuchika and was diligently raised as the first son of a samurai family.

People around the area said, "Yasuchika is such an open and energetic child, the Sugiyama family must be so happy!"

However, after he turned 7 years old, Yasuchika, who until that time had never been sick, contracted smallpox, an epidemic of which was spreading throughout the province. In those days many people died of smallpox, but thanks to his parents' devoted care, Yasuchika survived. However, as a result of the high fever he suffered, he lost his eyesight and became blind.

Caption:
A happy-looking Yasuchika being carried by his mother.

P2

"Oh, what a terrible thing to happen! If it was at all possible for me to take your place, I gladly would." Yasuchika's mother took him to see doctors who were said to specialize in eye problems and visited temples and shrines reputed to cure eye diseases. However, despite the desperate efforts and prayers of his parents, Yasuchika's vision was not restored.

Then one day, Shigemasa called for Yasuchika's mother and spoke to her.

"It was good that you helped Yasuchika as much as you could, but, being blind, it will be impossible for him to be the successor of a samurai household. One possibility would be to ask a Buddhist temple to accept him and let him become a monk, but....."

"What is best for him, I wonder?"

"It's not that our family wouldn't be able to care for one disabled son, but I wouldn't want him to live without having a purpose in life."

"I think so, too."

Caption:
As she watches over him, Yasuchika's mother asks the doctor to examine his eyes.

P3

Yasuchika's parents thought deeply about his future and decided, above all else, to develop his independence. They raised him strictly so he would have a mind that would not accept being pitied by people because he was blind.

First, they taught him how to dress himself properly and to learn how to behave so that he wouldn't be ridiculed by others.

However, Yasuchika couldn't always understand his parents' thinking and often asked them for help, saying,

"I can't see, so I can't do it."

But, Yasuchika's mother refused to help him and said,

"You must do it yourself, despite how long it takes. I'll teach you but I won't help you."

No matter how much Yasuchika cried or became angry, his parents refused to give in to him. It was their sincere hope that he would become the kind of person who could do things on his own.

Thanks to his parents' strict discipline and loving concern, Yasuchika gradually grew up stronger.

Caption:
(Upper right) Yasuchika as a child, crying and complaining.
(Lower left) Yasuchika is now able to change his clothes by himself.
(Center) Yasuchika has grown into an impressive son of a samurai.

P4

Eventually, when he turned 18, Yasuchika told his parents,

"As I am blind, I've given up the idea of following the way of a samurai, but neither do I have the confidence to play the koto or shamisen in front of people. Instead, I have learned that in Edo (present day Tokyo), there is a renowned blind acupuncturist called Yamase Takuichi and, if possible, I'd like to become his disciple and help people who are suffering from illness."

In those days, the work of blind people was mostly restricted to being a biwa player, a shamisen player or an anma masseuse. It was a time when there weren't many acupuncturists providing treatment. However, based on his experience of having received acupuncture when he had been sick in the past, Yasuchika professed his will to lay down the sword and live independently as a blind person by establishing himself in acupuncture.

"It seems you are so determined that you are even prepared to leave our house for good, therefore I won't stop you."

After obtaining his parents' permission, Yasuchika eventually made it to Edo, having encountered many hardships along the way. He visited the clinic of Yamase Takuichi in Atagoshita in the Shiba district (present day Minato Ward, Tokyo) and asked Yamase to accept him as a disciple.

At that time, there were very few blind acupuncturists and though Takuichi was called a "Master", he was still only about 30 years old himself. Moved by Yasuchika's sincere desire to use acupuncture to help people suffering from various diseases, Takuichi readily accepted him into his house. After that, Yasuchika changed his name to "Waichi" by adding "ichi", which was included in the names of blind biwa players at the time, and once more reaffirmed his determination.

Caption:
(Upper) Yasuchika imagines the universe of the human body spreading out from the meridian.
(Lower right) Relying on his cane, Yasuchika travels towards Edo.

P5

In those days, in order to study techniques, a disciple was called a "live-in disciple" and resided in the Master's house, taking care of many of the Master's daily needs, such as drawing water and cleaning. What's more, at that time, Waichi was the only live-in disciple in the house.

It was hard work receiving patients and doing cleaning, laundry and arranging the rooms all in a way that was different from what he was used to in his own home.

One day, Waichi was having a late dinner with his Master.

"Waichi, are you tired? Your work is messy and slow. Are you slacking off at the floor cleaning?"

"No, no. I don't mean to…."
"I may be blind but I have eyes in the soles of my feet. Don't lie!"
When he heard these words, Waichi realized that his Master was not only skilled in acupuncture techniques. From that day on, after cleaning the room, he always checked carefully with the palms of his hands or the soles of his feet that there was no dust left anywhere.

> Caption:
> Waichi wipes the long corridor by himself while his Master watches.

P6

A year passed in the blink of an eye. However, during that year Waichi had received very little in the way of introduction to acupuncture techniques. He often heard difficult acupuncture terms being spoken but, as this was in a time before Braille had been developed, he soon forgot them.

> Caption:
> Waichi attempts to perform acupuncture on his Master, but is so nervous that his hands won't move.

P7

As he entered his second year in the house, Waichi began to feel uneasy.
"Today was another day that the Master didn't teach me anything. I'm a live-in disciple in name only. Am I not just a handyman around here? But I made a firm commitment to my parents so I mustn't complain about it."
One day, early in the spring of his third year in the house, Waichi was suddenly called by his Master.
"I have some free time today, so how about trying some acupuncture on me?"
"What? On the Master's body?"
It was so sudden that, rather than being pleased, Waichi felt very nervous and his mind went blank.
"Master, you haven't taught me anything about acupuncture yet, so I don't think I can do it. Where should I put the needle?"
At that, the Master shouted at Waichi in a loud voice that he'd never heard before.
"What did you say? What do you mean I haven't taught you anything? Are you saying you've spent the last 3 years being unhappy that I make you do household chores every day?"
"No…."
He stammered and wished he hadn't spoken but the Master had seen into Waichi's heart.
"Every day, a lot of people come here to receive treatment and I have to deal with the patients and also treat them. You are living in this house so, every day from morning to night, you have endless opportunities to learn."
"……"
"The reason I get you to do the housework isn't just to use you as a handyman. No matter how good you are at acupuncture, you'll never be accepted in society if you aren't respected as a person."
Waichi was deeply ashamed at the foolishness of his outburst and thought carefully about his Master's words.
Acupuncture isn't easy as it is rooted in knowing the complex structure of the human body and the necessity to remember a lot of medical terminology. After that, his Master taught him a lot in a short time, but, in the end, Waichi found it hard to remember things. His Master had him practice using acupuncture needles on his body, but Waichi was so nervous that he couldn't perform it well. The Master began to feel worried about Waichi's future. However, feeling responsible for having taken in Waichi and the great dream he held, he tried his utmost to teach him the practical skills of acupuncture, but, rather than improving, Waichi found

himself falling behind disciples who had entered the school after him.

P8

One day, after 5 years as a live-in disciple, Waichi was called to his Master's room.
"Waichi. As I always intended, I've spent a long time guiding you, but I can do it no longer. No matter how much I teach you, it seems you'll never be able to perform acupuncture without causing pain. I acquired my techniques in my own way, but I don't have the skills that you desire. Though it might seem harsh, I want you to gather your things tomorrow, leave here and return to your parents' house."
Waichi was stunned at this sudden pronouncement and asked if there was no way that he could continue with his studies. However, his request was refused.
After a sleepless night, Waichi bid farewell to his Master the next morning.
"Waichi, I can't do it, but, depending on your own ingenuity, you should be able to develop the acupuncture skills you seek. Also, never forget your own efforts and the power of the gods."
"Thank you for taking care of me for so long."
Early in spring, at the beginning of April, Waichi wiped away his tears and left the house of the Master who had cared for him for the last 5 years. There was nobody to show him the way. He couldn't even return to his hometown now.
"Where should I go? What should I do?"
He was at a loss. Suddenly, Waichi remembered that his Master had said "the power of the gods" as he was leaving the house.
Waichi decided that there was nothing else for him to do but to go and pray at the shrine of Benten in Enoshima who had long been regarded as the guardian deity of blind people. Enoshima was a small island in Fujisawa town in the province of Sagami (present day Kanagawa Prefecture) but it was famous for being the location of one of Japan's 3 major Benten shrines and Benten was enshrined there as the goddess of manual techniques. However, Waichi didn't know the way to Enoshima. He decided he would set out using a wooden cane and head south, taking note of what people told him as he met them on the road. The streets of Edo were crowded and when he asked people the way, most of them kindly told him. There were even some who, on noticing he was blind, took him by the arm and led him in the right direction. On the other hand, there were also those who considered him a nuisance and shouted abuse at him, saying, "Oi, what are you doing wandering all over the road like that?"

> Caption:
> Waichi smiles as he eats a dinner prepared by the priest at a temple.

P9

The distance from Edo to Enoshima was about a dozen ri (50 kilometers). Though the Tokaido was a major route, at that time it was a bumpy path of heavily trampled earth and stones. What's more, it was very dangerous because of the many robbers who roamed the road.
As long as it didn't rain, Waichi walked with his cane during the day and stayed at cheap inns at night. But, in order to save the money he had received as a parting gift from his Master, eventually he began to ask if he could stay at shrines or temples along the way.
Sometimes his heart was gladdened when the priest at a temple provided him with dinner, or other times, a kind palanquin bearer would let him ride in the sedan chair for free. However, there were also occasions when he would lose his way and get chased off after asking for directions at a private house or he continued to walk in a storm, all the while fearing being struck by lightning. Some-

times, tripping over stones all day, the straw sandals he put on in the morning were in shreds by the evening.

P10

It took him 5 or 6 days to eventually reach Enoshima. He hadn't bathed and his clothes were in rags. People avoided him, saying, "What's wrong with that fellow. He really stinks!"
Still, encouraged by the thought of the goddess Benten ahead of him, Waichi began to climb the steep stone steps.
Eventually he reached the upper priest of the Nakatsu no Miya Shrine.
"Excuse me. I realize it's rather sudden, but I'm here to carry out fasting practice….."
Dressed in ragged clothes and with a torn umbrella, Waichi asked for guidance.
"What? You want to do fasting practice looking as dirty as this? Don't be ridiculous! Leave the island immediately!"
"But, I came all this way to ask you…."
Having no other choice, Waichi stumbled down the steep steps he had just climbed. He was barefoot and the soles of his feet were covered in cuts as his straw sandals had worn out. In this state, he wouldn't even be able to get off the island.

Caption:
    Waichi runs away from the priest who raises his hand and threatens him.

P11

It was then that Waichi heard a voice.
"What happened to you?"
"I'm sorry. Who is that?"
"I beg your pardon. I'm the lower priest, my name is Kyojunin."
"As you can see, I'm blind and I came here to pray to the goddess Benten for guidance on the best way for me to proceed as an acupuncturist, but I was scolded by the upper priest and had to leave."
"Well, well, you seem to be very strong in your conviction. The upper priest was rather rude…."
"I decided to come here to stay in a cave, practice fasting and beg to be enlightened about a new way of acupuncture, no matter how long it takes."
"If you don't mind, please come along with me. First, I'll take care of your injuries then I'll help you fulfill your wishes."

Caption:
    Kyojunin gently puts his hand to Waichi's ear and speaks softly to him.

P12

Maybe this was not an example of "if there is a god who throws away, there is a god who picks up", but surely, wasn't this a sign of the goddess Benten at work?
After having his feet treated by Kyojunin, Waichi entered into a cave on the coast and began his practice of fasting and praying.
With his body in a weakened state after his hard journey, fasting could have put his life in danger.
On the first and second days, his mind was easily distracted by various worries. On the third and fourth days he struggled against hunger. On the fifth and sixth days he was in an agony between life and death.
Then, on the seventh day, he felt a strange feeling of being released from all his worries, doubts and suffering.
On the morning of the eighth day, as the eastern sea turned a wild shade of red, a haziness came over Waichi's mind and body.
"Goddess Benten, I have continued my fasting for over a week but I have received neither strength nor any sign from you. I've come to think that it would be easier to throw myself into the sea and die

than to have to depend on the care of others for the rest of my life. I'm truly sorry that I haven't been able to live up to Kyojunin's kindness…."
In his heart, Waichi wept and apologized sincerely.

Caption:
    Waichi practices zazen meditation in the cave.

P13

Filled with sadness, Waichi felt for the wooden cane beside him, gripped it tightly, staggered out of the cave and began to walk on the rocks. At that point, he tripped over a large stone and fell.
"Ouch! What's this?"
Half-dazed, Waichi noticed something sharp had stuck into his foot. It was so painful that he sat down right there. Feeling it with his hand he found that a pine needle, wrapped in a cylindrically curled fallen leaf, had pierced his skin. He immediately pulled it out, but the next instant a thought flashed into his mind.
"That's it! If you put a needle inside a thin tube, you should be able to accurately stimulate acupuncture points. What a discovery! This must be a revelation from Benten!"
With his hopes rising, Waichi returned to the cave and prayed in thanks to the goddess.

Caption:
    A pine needle wrapped in a cylindrical leaf lies in Waichi's hand. Beyond that, an image of the goddess Benten appears.

P14

Though his body was so weak he could hardly walk, Waichi desperately stumbled over the rocks as he wanted to let Kyojunin know what he had discovered. When he reached the lower shrine, he suddenly heard his voice.
"Waichi, I haven't seen you for a long time. I was worried about you every day."
"Ah, Kyojunin! I have made a wonderful discovery! I had to come and tell you about it."
"Well, I'm very happy to hear that….."
Though he was on the point of collapsing, choking with happiness, Waichi explained in a rush all about the pine needle wrapped in a cylindrical leaf.
"That all may be so, but you are very weak from fasting. If it's OK with you, why don't you rest here for a while?"
Thanks to Kyojunin's care, Waichi's health rapidly recovered.

Caption:
    Waichi shows the pine needle to Kyojunin. The effects of the severity of his fasting practice are evident in the thinness of his body.

P15

When he was feeling better, Waichi returned to Edo and visited his Master, Yamase Takuichi, to tell him about his new acupuncture discovery. Yamase was very happy and pressed Waichi to develop his new technique and continue his acupuncture training at the clinic. Waichi immersed himself in developing this new method that would allow even blind people to easily and accurately apply the needles in acupuncture. He realized that, if he truly wanted to be able to treat the human body, he needed to study and practice more and more.
One day, about 5 years later, Yamase called for Waichi and said, "Waichi, when you came here, you were a young boy who knew nothing. Now, you have grown such that you could even take my place here. As a Master, I have nothing more to teach you. You should probably leave my side now and find a way to further deep-

en your studies."

Yamase decided to write a letter of introduction and send Waichi to visit his own Master, Irie Yoshiaki, in Kyoto. In order to become a true acupuncturist, Yamase wanted Waichi to learn various skills in Kyoto, as he himself had done.

Before leaving for Kyoto, Waichi once more visited Kyojunin on Enoshima.

"Thank you for always supporting me. Actually, to make this 'guide tube and needle' technique truly useful as a medical treatment, I believe I need to visit as many elders as possible and study from them."

"Where are you headed to?"

"To Kyoto where there are many famous Masters."

"I think this is a good idea as it's something you have decided yourself. I would only ask one thing, that you never forget the goddess Benten."

"Of course. I vow to face towards Enoshima every morning and join my hands in prayer."

"I, too, will pray that you achieve success in your new form of acupuncture."

Receiving Kyojunin's words of encouragement, Waichi thanked him for all his help, strapped his few belongings to his back, took his cane in his hand and set out for Kyoto.

Caption:
Waichi silently works on his acupuncture studies by himself.

P16

Heading down the Tokaido, he used a palanquin from Odawara to pass the checkpoint. Noticing that Waichi was blind, he was allowed to pass through more easily than he had expected.

The palanquin wasn't comfortable to ride in, but, compared to the speed at which Waichi could walk with his cane, it was much faster. However, he noticed that he now had less money than he thought.

He got out of the palanquin at Mishima and decided he would continue along the Tokaido only on foot. The road was littered with stones and again, catching his feet on them, the straw sandals he put on in the morning were in pieces by the evening and it was like walking barefoot.

During his long journey, Waichi was helped by the kindness of many people. Every morning when he awoke, he never forgot to face to the east, join his hands together and pray to the goddess Benten for his safe travels and to give thanks to Kyojunin.

Caption:
Before setting off on his travels, Waichi prays in the direction of the rising sun.

P17

However, a problem did arise. By the time he reached Lake Biwa, his physical strength had declined considerably as he had been saving money on lodgings and food. What's more, as he often slept in the open air, his clothing was in tatters and he looked like a beggar.

"Excuse me, I'm a traveler, could you......", he would say, but people passed him by, pretending not to notice.

Waichi's heart was often hurt as he heard loud voices exclaim,

"What a filthy thing!"

"He stinks, and on top of that, he's blind, too!"

Nevertheless, he continued to walk towards Kyoto, with a single-minded desire to develop his new method of acupuncture.

P18

He had no idea where he was or how he had walked there. He heard people talking to each other and apparently he had arrived in Omi (present day Shiga Prefecture), close to his hometown.

From somewhere, the delicious smells of someone cooking dinner wafted on the air. It made Waichi think of his parents and he couldn't hold back the tears. However, remembering the determination with which he had left his home, he knew there was no way that he could go back there.

When he eventually managed to reach Kyoto, Waichi finally collapsed in exhaustion.

"What's wrong? What is it? Who is this?"

"Oh, he's collapsed. What a stink!"

"I think this fellow's blind. It looks like he is exhausted from stumbling along with his cane!"

Many people had gathered around but they were just standing there and staring.

At that moment, several men and women rushed over from a nearby large house.

"What happened?"

"This man suddenly collapsed."

"What? That's terrible. Quick, call the Master."

A young man hurried back to the house and soon a very elegant gentleman appeared, took Waichi's arm and checked his pulse.

"His pulse is very weak. Bring my medical box, please."

The Master took out some acupuncture needles from the box and quickly began to apply them.

The onlookers watched fearfully, but eventually someone cried out in a surprised voice,

"Oh, he's alive! He's moving!"

"He's conscious but still very weak, so let's take care of him at the house for the time being."

Actually, this person was the famous Kyoto acupuncturist, Irie Toyoaki.

Caption:
Onlookers stand around watching as a man performs acupuncture on Waichi, who has collapsed in the street.

P19

What was even more surprising was that Toyoaki's father was Irie Yoshiaki, the person to whom Yamase Takuichi, who had taken care of Waichi in Edo, had written the letter of introduction.

"If I hadn't collapsed in front of Master Irie's house at that time, I probably would have died."

Waichi was thankful for having been lucky twice: once when he met Kyojunin and now when he was saved by Master Irie as he was on death's doorstep.

P20

Thanks to the kind care provided by the people at the Irie clinic, Waichi's condition improved day by day. As time went by, he realized what a great man Master Irie was and how he was respected by many people. He also noticed how his disciples were studying medicine even in their own time.

Every evening after the patients had left, the disciples gathered in a large room and reviewed the things the Master had taught them 3 times. If you repeat something 3 times, strangely enough, even Waichi could remember it. He reflected on the serious attitude of these disciples and how he had been so easily satisfied until now.

When Waichi's physical condition had recovered, the Master asked him,

"So, what are you planning to do from now on?"

He responded by honestly expressing his feelings,

"I realize it's selfish of me, but would you accept me as a live-in disciple here?"

"Ah, so that's what you've been thinking. However, I heard that you are developing a new method of acupuncture. What is your main motive for wanting to study here?"

"Well, since I've been here under your care, two things have made

a very strong impression on me. First, you treat patients only after you have checked the condition of the whole body. The second is that your disciples are able to perfectly understand very difficult medical texts, and yet, they continue to study deeply every day."
"I see. Well, you need to be aware that I won't give you any special treatment. Are you able to put aside the fact that you are blind?"
"Yes."
"This place is much stricter than Master Yamase Takuichi's clinic in Edo. This work involves taking people's lives in our hands so, first, you must concentrate on honing your personality and acquiring treatment skills which are second to none."

Caption:
    A silhouette of Waichi sincerely facing Master Irie as he is warned of the conditions he must follow at the house.

P21

At Master Yamase's clinic, Waichi had woken up at 5 a.m. every morning. However, here at the Irie school, all the disciples were ready to start their own work before 5 a.m. Everyone was working quietly, sharing out the jobs such as tending the garden, cleaning inside the house and preparing breakfast. Waichi was given a cloth to clean the hallway floors. It was more difficult than he thought because the house was so big. Before long, he was also given the job of wiping the sliding doors and screens and even the bathroom. Every day, after more than 2 hours of cleaning, the quality of his workmanship was inspected by the senior disciples. After the day's work and clearing away the dinner things, they all spent a little time in deep discussion about the patients who had visited that day and their treatment.
"Every day, it's none stop here, isn't it…..", Waichi thought.
He was full of admiration for the others, but he also found that he was much more able to remember things now than he had been before.

Caption:
    The disciples sit in a circle discussing enthusiastically.

P22

The Master and the disciples worked together and spent a lot of time enthusiastically teaching Waichi. However, no matter how hard he tried, Waichi was unable to perform acupuncture well. His fellow disciples even acted as patients for him to practice on, but just saying
 "Ouch! It hurts!" didn't help him improve his treatment techniques.
"It's difficult for everyone. Even Master Irie said that it took him decades before he could perform acupuncture the way he wanted to."
Waichi's fellow disciples had these kind words for him as he felt he was losing confidence.
"The way of acupuncture is like walking steadily along a mountain path, following tiny lights that can be seen in the far distance."
"Now that you are practicing here, when you are working close to the Master as he is treating patients, listen very carefully to what he is saying. A disciple is especially privileged to be able to do this."
Waichi thanked his colleagues for their advice and decided he would follow it immediately.
The Master's treatment room was a simple area, separated by just one sliding door, however it was usually quiet and not a single sound could be heard during a session. A certain nervousness could be sensed in the responses when the Master occasionally spoke to the patient as he treated them. However, eventually, when the treatment was finished, the patient would thank the Master in a cheerful voice. At that point the Master said,

"Please get well soon. Thank you very much."
Waichi was surprised to hear the Master thank the patient.
"Ah, I see. We mustn't think of this work as us just providing the treatment," Waichi thought to himself.
In addition to acquiring the knowledge and skills of treatment, he also grew to greatly appreciate the wonderful humanity of his Master.
One day, the Master left it to Waichi to treat a patient who was close to recovery.
"Oh, that hurts!"
It seems he couldn't do it well after all.
"I beg your pardon. It's my fault. Please forgive me. I'll treat you from now on."
The patient readily agreed with the Master's words.

Caption:
    Acupuncture needles used in the treatment room.

P23

That night, after the patients had all returned home, the Master called Waichi to his room.
"It's now 7 years since you first came here. You have been taught the theory and techniques of the Irie-style of acupuncture and, though your theoretical studies have progressed smoothly, it seems that understanding the secrets of the techniques is still difficult for you. I admire your enthusiasm, but I think our style of acupuncture isn't suitable for you as a blind person. To perfect acupuncture techniques which are more befitting someone who is completely blind, further development is necessary. With that in mind, what do you think about studying with another Master in Kyoto to develop the new style of acupuncture that you are working on?"
The Master didn't say the word "expelled", but Waichi understood what he had said.
"I'll do as the Master says."
The next morning, Waichi thanked his Master for saving his life and for teaching him many things, including the secrets of the Irie-style of acupuncture. He apologized for being unable to fully respond to his teaching. He also asked him for an introduction to a senior Master in Kyoto and said he was determined to continue his medical studies.
"That's good. If you have the will to learn, you'll definitely understand everything. I will never forget you. I pray for your success with the guide tube method of acupuncture."
With deep appreciation for the magnitude of Master Irie's humanity, Waichi left the house.

Caption:
    Waichi bids farewell to Master Irie at the doorway.

P24

Waichi went on to become a disciple to Misono Isai and various other famous influential acupuncture doctors in Kyoto, gaining knowledge and studying the treatment styles of each of his senior teachers.
By the time Waichi finally managed to perfect his own method of treatment, he was in his 40s.
"Right, I'll go back to Edo and open my own facility," he thought to himself.
Waichi established a clinic in Kojimachi, near Edo Castle (present day Chiyoda Ward, Tokyo). He opened a private school inside his residence and called it the Sugiyama School. First he went to visit Yamase Takuichi, who had taken care of him many years before.
"I always knew you were a person who would achieve great things….."
Takuichi was as happy as he could have been, and he congratulated Waichi with all his heart as he left the house.
Until then, acupuncture treatment was often painful for patients as

it used the Chinese style of thick needles inserted by hand. However, the guide tube technique devised by Waichi was much less painful and very effective.

"The acupuncture in Kojimachi works really well and it isn't as painful as it used to be."

The reputation of the clinic grew as patients spoke about it and, before long, the name of the guide tube technique had spread not only in Edo but as far as the northern Kansai region.

Waichi never let this praise go to his head.

"I'm still learning….", he would say and whenever he had some spare time, he devoted himself day and night to completing his development of the guide tube technique based on the knowledge he had gained in Kyoto.

Caption:
Waichi practices his "guide tube" method of acupuncture, applying a needle through a tube to the patient's body.

P25

The guide tube method of acupuncture treatment devised by Waichi involved inserting a thin needle into a tube. The thin bamboo initially used for the guide was easy to come by but tended to wither and break easily. After considering various options, Waichi hit on the idea that a thin metal tube would be the best solution. However, in order for this to work, he would need the cooperation of a highly skilled craftsman who could roll metal into a thin cylindrical shape.

The next task was the needles. At that time, needles used in acupuncture were called "twisting needles" and were thicker at the base so that they wouldn't bend when they were inserted directly into the skin and twisted. In order for the needle to pass through the tube, the needle needed to be the same thickness from the base to the sharp tip, like a pine needle. It was necessary to develop a new acupuncture needle resembling a pine needle.

What's more, it was necessary to devise a way to have the needle pass through the tube and be inserted into the body. For this, inspiration could be found in the "tapped needle" method developed in Japan in which the head of the needle was lightly hit with a small hammer. A technique was devised whereby, instead of using a hammer, the head of the needle could be lightly tapped with the fingertips to push the tip of the needle out of the tube and painlessly into the skin.

The "guide tube acupuncture" developed in this way attracted attention not only from blind practitioners but also from normally-sighted acupuncturists as it allowed for fine needles to be inserted accurately into the acupuncture points without pain.

But that wasn't all. Waichi worked hard to improve the effectiveness of the treatment and he managed to devise and perfect 100 different acupuncture techniques.

Fortunately, at that time, substantial amounts of silver and gold were being produced from the Iwami silver mine in Izumo (present day Shimane Prefecture) and the Sado gold mine in Echigo (present day Niigata Prefecture). The silver and gold needed for acupuncture needles were readily available, so excellent new tubes and needles were developed one after another and their reputation spread throughout Japan.

P26

At this point, let's mention a mutual aid society for the blind called "Todoza". In the Edo period, it was common for blind men to pay a fee to become members of a guild called "Todoza".

In this guild (somewhat similar to the present day welfare and pension system), there were hierarchical ranks, such as "kengyo", "betto", "koto" and "zato". These were awarded for excellence, but, later, could also could be purchased for a fee. The collected money was then distributed amongst the members depending on the rank.

On New Year's Day 1670 (Kanbun 10), Waichi was awarded the rank of "kengyo". The position of "kengyo" was the highest of the 73 ranks in the guild. The majority of the members of "Todoza" were teachers of musical instruments such as the koto, the shamisen and the biwa. That an acupuncturist achieved the highest rank was due to the excellent reputation of the Sugiyama School's "guide tube" method and also the recognition of Waichi's sincere and gentle personality.

Waichi's reputation grew and eventually the leaders of the Shogunate in Edo expressed strong interest in his methods.

Caption:
Waichi is seated in his role of "kengyo".

P27

In 1680 (Enpo 8), Waichi was contacted by Inoue Gentetsu , the doctor who looked after the Shogun's family. He said the condition of the fourth Shogun, Tokugawa Ietsuna, was causing concern. Waichi was also troubled as the Shogun's symptoms were unexpectedly bad. As a result of Waichi's dedicated treatment, the pain was temporarily relieved and the palace attendants were very happy. However, kengyo Waichi could see that the condition of the Shogun was serious.

"I am glad that you contacted me at this time. Acupuncture will temporarily improve the Shogun's blood circulation and it may appear that his condition has become much better, however the passage of the next month will be most difficult."

The attendants were momentarily surprised at this, but unfortunately Waichi's diagnosis was correct. One month later, on May 8th, despite the treatment, Shogun Ietsuna's short life came to an end at the age of 40.

Caption:
Waichi places his hand on the body of Shogun Tokugawa Ietsuna as he diagnoses him.

P28

On the other hand, the Sugiyama School was becoming very popular as a clinic. When they opened the doors in the morning, there was always a line of patients already waiting. It became difficult for the totally blind Waichi to handle everything himself and he needed to find somebody to help him, so he decided to ask for help in finding a maid to do the housework. Very soon he was introduced to a woman named Setsu. She was young, intelligent and good-natured and she ended up working at the Sugiyama School.

A typical day at the Sugiyama School began at 5 a.m. After taking care of Waichi, Setsu worked hard at everything, from the cleaning, laundry and cooking to preparing the treatment room. The Sugiyama School was doing very well and Setsu became indispensable to the patients.

"Thank you, Setsu. Hard workers like you are rare. I'm very happy to have met such a good person."

"Not at all. We still have a long way to go. Please ask me for anything, I'm at your service."

"Thank you. Actually, I do have a favor to ask of you. I'd like you to take me to Enoshima once a month."

"I shall be very glad to accompany you as you request."

Caption:
Setsu diligently doing the cleaning, washing, serving etc.

P29

After that, no matter how busy he was, Waichi visited Enoshima every month without fail to give thanks to the goddess Benten for helping him develop the guide tube method of acupuncture. After praying to the goddess on their first visit to Enoshima, Waichi showed Setsu the cave where he came up with the idea for his method.

"Setsu, this is where my life started."

"Master, I have heard you talk of this many times before, but now, for the first time, I really understand your deep feelings about this place."

The sight of Waichi standing quietly on the rocky ground, humming intently to himself, triggered a strange feeling in Setsu and she determined that, hereafter, she would devote her life to his service.

On the way back, Waichi visited Kyojunin. He told him how he prayed to the goddess Benten every morning, that he was thankful for all the kindness Kyojunin had shown him and also how helpful it was for the Sugiyama School to have the wonderfully understanding Setsu by his side.

After that, with his special devotion to the goddess Benten, Waichi arranged to have 48 milestones constructed on the road from Fujisawa to Enoshima to make it easier for blind people and other devotees to visit the shrine to Benten. In addition, he also had a warning lantern built on the coast of the cape to help protect fishermen from accidents.

P30

In 1682 (Tenna 2), the 72-year old Waichi established a vocational school for the visually-impaired called the "Acupuncture Treatment Training School". The science and techniques of acupuncture, primarily the guide tube method invented by Waichi, moxibustion and anma massage were taught at the school. This was the precursor to what later became the "Acupuncture and Anma Teacher Training School For The Blind." That such a place was created more than 100 years before Valentin Hauy established the first school for the visually-impaired in Europe in 1784 was truly something to be proud of before the world.

Waichi's principle disciple, Mishima Yasuichi, and others, later opened 45 of these schools throughout Japan, primarily a school at the juncture of each of the 4 main highways into Edo, at Shinagawa, Shinjuku, Itabashi and Senju. These 45 became the basis of the present day network of prefectural schools for the blind.

With the location of the schools decided, Waichi began writing textbooks for use in training the students.

In order to accurately convey the theories and techniques of acupuncture to future generations, Waichi felt that, rather than using word-of-mouth as had been done until now, textbooks and education were important for this to be accepted as an academic subject. His dream was to teach his students treatment methods using guidance books written by himself. He aimed to create vocational education for the visually-impaired that would allow them to establish their independence in the world as acupuncturists.

Caption:
The signboard of the "Acupuncture Treatment Training School" outside a detached house.

P31

Waichi was blind, so writing wasn't an option for him (it wasn't until 150 years later that Louis Braille in France invented his marvelous system of reading and writing for the visually-impaired).

At first, he asked Setsu to take dictation from him. However, he soon realized that it was difficult for her as there were many technical acupuncture terms in his instructions. He asked his friends and acquaintances for help in finding a suitable person for the task, but even in a city as big as Edo, it wasn't easy to locate such a person.

It needed someone with medical expertise to be able to write down in kanji the many difficult terms unique to acupuncture. Even

though Waichi himself knew the words, he was at a loss when asked what the correct kanji were. Once again, he realized how difficult it was to produce a specialized guidance manual for acupuncturists and it left him feeling troubled.

Still, Waichi wasn't discouraged. Every evening, after treating his patients, he worked late into the night creating the guidance manual.

His mind was filled with ideas and he realized that the most important thing was to get them down on paper. This thought made him feel better and he decided that he would have Setsu write things down for him until he could find a suitable specialist.

As expected, Setsu was reluctant, saying it wasn't possible, but Waichi wouldn't give up.

"Just write down what I say in hiragana. That will be fine."

In the end, Setsu accepted the Master's sincere request.

From the following day, after the usual daily work was finished, she took down Waichi's dictation. With this, it seems that the Master's mind became more organized and good ideas came to him one after another.

"Setsu, your cooperation is truly a great help. Words are very important in this world, but if they are not recorded in writing, they will just disappear."

"Master, what you say is absolutely true. I'm very happy that I can be of even the slightest help to you."

Caption:
Setsu listens to Waichi's dictation and writes down his words one by one.

P32

The Sugiyama School was filled with patients every day. Nevertheless, despite his busy schedule, Waichi continued to devote himself to finalizing the techniques of the guide tube method of acupuncture and completion of the guidance manuals. Not long after, a first draft of the medical textbook called "Sugiyama-ryu Sanbusho" *—The Sugiyama-Style Trilogy— was produced.

Acupuncture training schools were officially recognized as academic institutions by the Shogunate and with the completion of the guidance manual, they were able to attract many excellent applicants. Until then, the only way for a Master to teach his apprentice was to rely on memory. However, now there was a guidance manual in every acupuncture training school. People were very impressed by Waichi's advanced way of thinking.

* The first part of the trilogy was "Ryoji no Taigaishu"— A General Manual of Acupuncture Therapy. With the cooperation of the Shogunate's medical officers, all the original kana transcriptions of medical jargon, such as disease names and acupuncture points, had been changed to kanji characters and the book was organized in short sentences so that blind people could easily memorize them. The second part was "Senshin Sanyoshu"—The Three Essentials of Acupuncture—a collection of important theories of acupuncture mentioned in Chinese classical literature and written in Chinese characters. The third part was "Igaku Setsuyoshu"—A Compilation of Medical Sections—a general introduction to Oriental medicine, which was compiled by his disciples after Waichi's death and used as a lecture guide in the Acupuncture Training Schools.

Caption:
The "Sugiyama-Style Trilogy" is bound with string and ready to be used as a guidance manual.

P33

In his position as "kengyo", Waichi was busy every day with acupuncture treatment and also interactions with members of the Shogunate government. However, as full as his schedule was, Waichi considered his next job to be raising excellent disciples from among the blind, like himself. At that time, the majority of blind people made a living from playing the koto or the shamisen. Some followed the path of anma massage. Few chose the technically difficult way of acupuncture. Among the former were people who heard how well the Sugiyama School was doing and wanted to become disciples there, simply thinking that it would make them more prosperous. When such people visited the school, Waichi strongly reproached them.

"It would seem that you have travelled from far away to Edo, but I must tell you that I am not looking for disciples who just want to get rich. Practicing the guide tube method of acupuncture is a lifelong commitment to improving your techniques to help people suffering from disease."

For example, the following happened. A father brought his son, who was blind from birth, to the school and asked Waichi to accept him as a disciple .

He said, "I can make a donation….."

"I'm not doing this work to make money! It's the worse thing to practice acupuncture with such impure motives, go home!"

Like a raging fire, the usually gentle Waichi angrily sent him away. When selecting a disciple, Waichi put much more value on a student's personality than on their comprehension or skills. Among the many applicants to the school, the ones chosen were all outstanding people, even if they were blind. Eventually, one after another, the best disciples from this school achieved their independence and went on to become active in their local areas.

Caption:
Waichi angrily shakes his fist at a father who offered a donation to have his son accepted as a disciple.

P34

Regarding the government, after the death of the 4th Shogun, Ietsuna, his half-brother Tsunayoshi had become the 5th Shogun at the age of 35. Tsunayoshi showed a great interest in learning, was a keen scholar and stated that he wouldn't tolerate corruption among government officials, but on the other hand, in some ways he was also rather timid.

One time, feeling frustration at having become Shogun, Tsunayoshi stabbed one of his retainers. This incident caused Tsunayoshi to become mentally unstable. In those days, what we know as "neurosis" was called "dancing sickness" by people. When it was noticed by his retainers that Tsunayoshi had been afflicted by this disease, they asked for Waichi's help in treating him.

At first, Tsunayoshi seemed unhappy about this, but after Waichi began the acupuncture treatment, he relaxed and fell into a peaceful sleep. After the treatment was finished, one of the retainers spoke to Tsunayoshi in a quiet voice and he was like a different person. The tense, nervous expression he had shown before had disappeared and his face appeared calm.

"After a few more treatments, I'm sure you'll get better."

Soon, Tsunayoshi's mental illness was completely cured. The Shogun was very pleased and gave Waichi a large monetary reward as well as granting him a monthly salary as a court physician and even arranged a mansion for him in Otemachi. It's easy to see how well Waichi was treated.

Waichi didn't let the courtesy of the Shogun go to his head. In fact, he wished for the happiness of the Shogun's family with all his heart and secretly visited the lower shrine on Enoshima every month to pray for their well-being. This eventually came to the notice of the Shogunate officials and all concerned were moved to tears in gratitude for Waichi's sincerity.

His achievements were highly praised and not only was he promoted from gokenin (the lowest rank of vassal in the Shogun's household) to hatamoto (the highest ranking samurai in direct service of the Shogun), but, in 1689 (Genroku 2), he was also given a site of 500 tsubo (about 1600 square meters) in Ogawamachi. When Waichi was over 80 years old, in recognition of his age and

hard work, the Shogun allowed him to use a palanquin to access as far as the inner sanctum of Edo Castle.

Caption:
Waichi performs acupuncture on Shogun Tokugawa Tsunayoshi.

P35

At the age of 81, Waichi contracted a serious illness. Setsu was worried about him and, when she felt that his condition had eased a little, she rushed to Enoshima to pray to Benten.

"Dear Goddess, please find a way to cure the Master's illness. If you save his life, I promise to give this body to you."

Did Setsu's impassioned prayer have an effect? Well, Waichi miraculously recovered.

Nobody was happier about this than Setsu, but soon, perhaps in fulfillment of her promise to the goddess Benten, she threw herself into the sea off Enoshima and ended her life.

How did Waichi react when he learned of Setsu's sudden death? He felt deeply thankful for her life of dedicated hard work, but was left at a loss at this tragic parting.

"When I die, I want a grave to be built for Setsu next to mine. I'll never forget her."

He gave this instruction to his disciples with his heart full of love for Setsu.

Caption:
In his mind's eye, Waichi sees an image of a peaceful-looking Setsu joining her hands in prayer.

P36

The following year, in 1692 (Genroku 5), at the age of 82, Waichi was appointed to the rank of sokengyo for the Kanto region by order of the Shogun Tsunayoshi. This position was chairman of the highest ranks in the "Todoza" guild for blind people. How happy Setsu would have been if she had lived to see it.

In fulfillment of his responsibilities as sokengyo, Waichi carried out extensive organizational reforms of the "Todoza". By clarifying the disordered codes, or rules, pertaining to the different occupations represented in the guild, including not only acupuncturists and anma masseuses, but also koto and biwa players and moneylenders, he provided a concrete path to a livelihood for blind people.

One day, Shogun Tsunayoshi called for Waichi.

"Old man, it seems you are still visiting the goddess Benten on Enoshima every month."

"Yes, I intended to continue doing so as long as I was able to walk, but recently, no doubt due to my age, it feels more and more difficult."

"The sokengyo's sincere devotion is truly admirable, but do you think there might be another way?"

"Another way?"

"Well, I've prepared this."

The Shogun instructed one of his attendants to bring a paulownia wood box, about 1 meter long, and place it in front of Waichi.

"I had this made out of my deep feelings for you. First, I'd like you to gently feel it."

Waichi carefully touched the white cloth covering the object in the box and immediately understood.

"It believe its a very impressive statue, but…"

"As I expected, you have a keen sense. This is a golden statue of the goddess Benten. You should have it placed in a nearby temple and, instead of going to Enoshima, you can pray to her there."

Then he asked the sokengyo,

"I'll also reward you for everything you have done for me so far. Tell me what it is you want most just now."

Deeply moved and grateful for this kind consideration, Waichi was

determined to decline the offer, but said to the Shogun,
"Well, I suppose there must be one thing…."
Finally, he reluctantly began to speak.

Caption:
Seated next to the golden statue of the goddess Benten, Tokugawa Tsunayoshi offers to reward Waichi for his efforts. Waichi listens gratefully to his words.

P37

"Sir, I know it's clearly impossible, but I'd really like one eye (hitotsume)."
"What? You want one eye!?"
As was to be expected, this left the Shogun somewhat at a loss, but a few days later, a reply was delivered.
"I'll grant your request for one eye."
With that, he presented Waichi with a piece of land measuring 3000 tsubo (about 10,000 square meters) in an area known as Hitotsume (present day Chitose, Sumida Ward, Tokyo).
Waichi was very impressed by the Shogun's quick-wittedness and said,
"Sir, I am deeply grateful for all the things you have given me. I want to use this land for the people of the world, not just for myself."
To which the Shogun replied,
"Actually, the reason I gave the golden Benten statue to you was, I thought that if you built a shrine to Benten on the Hitotsume site and enshrined the statue there, you would more easily be able to pray to the goddess every day."
Before long, work on constructing the Benten shrine to hold the golden statue was begun.
"I am a blind man so I can't give you detailed instructions, but can you please build a shrine that will make the goddess Benten happy?"
Waichi's words went straight to the chief carpenter's heart and he worked diligently on the construction. The tone of the completed Benten shrine was quietly dignified rather than luxurious.
Rumors of the golden Benten statue spread throughout Edo and every day, many people came to pray. The number of pilgrims arriving by boat from Komagata also increased and it became famous as the "Hitotsume Benten of Edo". The Hitotsume site was also known as the Souroku Mansion and for over 100 years it was home to a government office for the blind and an acupuncture training center.
Shogun Tsunayoshi was known for having issued the evil "Law of Compassion for Living Creatures" which particularly included the strict protection of dogs. However, that also eventually led to the protection of socially vulnerable people such as infants, the elderly and the disabled. It is less well known that his encounter with Sugiyama Waichi played a major role in improving the social status of the blind.

P38

In 1694 (Genroku 7), Waichi turned 84 years old, but his research into acupuncture never lessened. His daily routine consisted of taking the Shogun's pulse, performing acupuncture and visiting the goddess Benten to pray.
The image of Waichi devoutly praying in the red robe specially approved by the Shogun displayed to all around the quiet dignity of a man who had achieved the peak of his ambitions and a presence that put people in mind of a god or buddah. Also, everyone was impressed that Waichi still spared a little time each day to continue his studies and there was unanimous praise for the effectiveness of his treatment.
The Shogun, born with a weak body, had always placed great faith in Waichi's character and treatment, even after his mental illness had been cured. However, even Waichi could not beat back the ever-approaching waves of old age and, on May 20th, like a large decaying tree, he fell into an everlasting sleep, ending a full life of 84 years.
Watched over by his faithful disciples, a solemn funeral was held at Miroku Temple in Tatekawa, Sumida Ward. A grave was built there and, along with the accompanying Acupuncture Needle Memorial Tower, it is now one of Tokyo's historical sites.
The following year, in 1695 (Genroku 8), a tomb was constructed below Hetsumiya Shrine on Enoshima and he was reburied there. Also, in accordance with Waichi's will, a tomb for Setsu was built alongside his grave.
After that, times changed and the land given to Waichi was confiscated by the Meiji government, and the acupuncture training center that had been moved from Waichi's private residence was closed, but the Benten shrine survived, cared for to this day by acupuncturists and the visually-impaired, as Ejima Sugiyama Shrine.
In 2016, around the 400th anniversary of his birth, a memorial hall was built on the grounds of the Shrine that houses materials related to Waichi's life. It offers a warm welcome to all those who respect Waichi. The hall also contains the "Sugiyama Acupuncture Center" where both normal-sighted and visually-impaired acupuncturists carry out treatment on a rotation basis.
The "guide tube method" of acupuncture, developed with considerable effort by Waichi, was well received by the general public because of its outstanding features. These days, acupuncturists are state-qualified medical professionals. Waichi's dream of securing a career path for the blind has become a reality.

Caption:
The Ejima Sugiyama Shrine exists to this day in Chitose, Sumida Ward, Tokyo.